First Special Report

The Defence Committee published its Third Report of Session 2003–04 on Lessons of Iraq as HC 57 on 16 March 2004. The Government's response to this report was received on 14 May 2004. It is set out below.

Government response

1. We very much welcome the House of Commons Defence Committee's report "*Lessons of Iraq*". It is right and important that Parliamentarians with experience of Defence carefully examine the performance of Britain's Armed Forces and civilians during high-intensity warfare at large scale. It is also proper for them to examine such areas as procurement, training and logistics, where work carried out previous to the campaign had a strong bearing on its successful outcome. We also value the Committee's investigation into our performance during the period subsequent to major combat operations.

2. The report covers a large range of areas and presents 131 conclusions and recommendations. These conclusions are generally positive. Some of the issues covered are both detailed and technical. But in assessing the Operation overall, we very much welcome the Committee's conclusion that: "The men and women of the Armed Forces deserve the highest praise for their conduct and performance in Iraq. The commitment required of them not only during the combat operations but also in the subsequent peacekeeping and peace support roles is of a very high order."

3. This memorandum sets out below the Government's response to each of the main points of Committee's report in the order in which they were raised.

The men and women of the Armed Forces deserve the highest praise for their conduct and performance in Iraq. The commitment required of them not only during the combat operations but also in the subsequent peacekeeping and peace support roles is of a very high order. (Paragraph 1).

4. We agree with the Committee.

We extend our deepest sympathies to the families of those who lost their lives. (Paragraph 1).

5. We thank the Committee for its sympathies, which have been passed to the Service Casualty Organisations.

We welcome the openness of MOD and the Armed Forces in publishing its 'lessons learned' reports on operations in Iraq and we commend them for the efforts they made to do so promptly after the major combat phase had concluded. (Paragraph 6).

6. We welcome the Committee's conclusion.

We regret that MOD has failed to provide us with certain documents which we have requested and has demonstrated on occasion less co-operation and openness than we

have the right to expect as a select Committee of the House of Commons. (Paragraph 21).

7. The Secretary of State has written to the Committee on this issue. We believe that the information that we withheld could not have been released without endangering current or future operations; nor do we agree with the Committee's conclusion in paragraph 21 that we could have released Commanding Officers' confidential accounts of the operation without endangering the candour of future accounts.

Special Forces

The 'increasing role' of Special Forces was demonstrated in operations in Afghanistan, and has now been emphatically reinforced by the crucial role which they played in Iraq. Their skills and professionalism provide a unique capability to the total British military effort. (Paragraph 23).

8. We agree that the Special Forces provide a unique capability to the total British military effort. We continue to invest in improving their capability through our Departmental Planning processes.

Planning and Strategy

The Debate within the Pentagon

The British, who had had embedded staff officers at Centcom from September 2001, were the first foreigners to be brought into the American planning process and appear to have been influential in the overall shape of the plan. In this the British-American relationship also drew on more than 10 years of close collaboration between the RAF and USAF in enforcing the northern and southern no-fly zones over Iraq. We are not, however, able to define the areas in which the British made specific contribution to what was essentially an American campaign plan, other than in the consideration of the northern option and in niche capabilities such as special forces operations. (Paragraph 43).

9. The Department believes that the contribution made by embedded UK officers was influential in the overall shape of the plan. Bilateral engagement between Commander CENTCOM and the UK Chief of Joint Operations provided the most effective and immediate path of influence throughout the planning stages. Below this, the UK had two principal liaison officers fully engaged at the military-strategic and operational levels of command: CDS' Liaison Officer in the Pentagon, and the Senior British Military Adviser and his staff at CENTCOM. The final plan was therefore the product of both US and UK thinking, discussion and ideas.

Effect of Operation FRESCO

Although the Armed Forces commitment to Operation FRESCO did not prevent them from putting together an effective force package for the operation in Iraq, it did limit the total numbers. It also adversely affected some elements of the force (by for example requiring high readiness units to move at short notice from fire- fighting to deploying

to Iraq). In the longer term it could have undermined the Armed Forces' ability to sustain combat operations. (Paragraph 56).

10. At the time of planning Operation TELIC the main effort for the Armed Forces was Operation FRESCO. However, the firefighting cover provided by the UK Armed Forces did not affect their ability to mount Operation TELIC. Obviously, if other commitments had not existed, the range of potential force packages would have been greater. That is always true. However, it does not follow that a different force package would have been better.

11. The air and maritime packages were in line with our Defence Planning Assumptions for an operation of this magnitude. They also provided specialist capabilities which add particular value to US forces, such as Air-to-Air Refuelling and Mine Counter Measures. Choosing the land component was more complicated because of the switch from planned operations in the North to South, which required an additional brigade—16 Air Assault Brigade—to strengthen our land assault capability. As a precaution we had made this possible by releasing the brigade from Operation FRESCO before Christmas.

Overall, the demands that Operation TELIC placed on UK Armed Forces in the context of other operational requirements were very close to the maximum that they could sustain. (Paragraph 57).

12. We accept that the requirement to support civilian authorities in the context of the firefighter strikes at the same time as the build up to hostilities in Iraq did place significant demands on our Armed Forces. These were, however, within our capabilities. When Operation FRESCO ended, further troops became available and this pressure was relieved.

13. The recent Defence White Paper acknowledged the additional demands placed on our Armed Forces by the range of expanding tasks and the level and frequency of operational deployments. Our planning assumptions have been revised accordingly and we intend to ensure that the Armed Forces are appropriately balanced for the challenges they are likely to face.

Planning Assumptions

We believe that MOD should consider whether for major equipment and capabilities the planning assumptions process is sufficiently flexible to match the very wide range of types and scales of operations which our Armed Forces may be required to undertake in the future. (Paragraph 59).

14. Planning assumptions are used to inform the development of the future structure of the Armed Forces to enable them best to meet the likely challenges of the future. In contrast to the Cold War, today's planning assumptions require flexible Armed Forces to meet a wide range of military tasks across different regions and environments. They are the result of a lengthy process of analysis of the future strategic environment that culminated in the publication of the Defence White Paper. They are guidelines—we may be able to do more from within the force structure, accepting that this will stretch personnel and resources, or we may choose to do less.

15. We need to strike the right balance between the programmed procurement of equipment and the purchase of equipment for specific operations as the result of an Urgent Operational Requirement (UOR). We should have equipment that is appropriate to the demands of the most likely and most frequent types of operation. It would be very costly, however, to hold a stockpile of equipment that is reserved solely for use on less frequent or likely operations. The UOR process is there to meet any shortfall and we need to ensure that it is responsive enough to meet the demands of operations that we might conduct with longer warning times.

The Northern option to the Southern option

From the evidence we have seen it appears that the late decision to move from the north to the south led to a requirement for the UK to deploy a significantly larger force—at least one brigade, something over 5,000 troops. This may well have been a contributory factor in complicating the various logistical problems that were later faced. (Paragraph 69).

16. The Committee correctly notes that following the decision to switch from the North to the South we judged we needed an additional brigade—16 Air Assault Brigade in this case. It is also possible that we would have required an additional brigade for the Northern Option, because of changes to the likely disposition of US forces under that option.

17. The additional troops required for the Southern Option did present a more challenging logistic supply task in volume terms. But while the Southern option resulted in a longer sea line of communication than the Northern option, both the land and sea lines of communication were easier to manage. Additionally, we were able to rationalise some elements of our structure by sharing some US logistic support there. Overall the Ministry of Defence is of the view that the challenges posed by mounting the Southern operation at relatively short notice were met, and that this was considerable achievement by our Armed Forces.

The Force Balance

MOD needs to urgently re-examine the mechanisms, including the use of reserves, by which units are brought to war establishment with minimal disruption in all important preparatory phases of the operations. (Paragraph 71).

18. The Army is already working through the "force generation" issues highlighted by Operation TELIC and experience on other recent operations. The outcome of this work will be the Future Army Structure, which was noted in the Defence White Paper (para 4.12). A formal announcement is expected later this year but options include closer integration between the Reserves and Regular forces and re-balancing manpower better to deliver the deployable element of the Army.

Overall, however, the signs are that, above Brigade level (i.e. at Division level), UK Armed Forces have become a one operation force—one operation which must be followed by a lengthy period of recovery before they can be in position to mount another similar operation, even within a Coalition. (Paragraph 74).

19. In the context of other commitments including Operation FRESCO, the demands of Operation TELIC were close to the top end of the spectrum of what we might expect the Armed Forces to be able to achieve. But this level of commitment reflects current Defence Policy, which is based upon developments and evidence since the SDR and its New Chapter, and the security challenges we foresee in the future.

20. The Defence White Paper described how the MOD plans to operate in the future strategic environment, countering the threats of WMD proliferation and international terrorism and addressing the challenges of weak and failing states. It is explicit about the scale of forces we require for the types of expeditionary operation that we should plan to undertake. It concluded that we need flexible Armed Forces that are structured and equipped for the most likely and most frequent types of operation at small and medium scale, in other words up to brigade level for the land component, while also meeting our Standing Tasks and Commitments.

21. Given time to prepare, the Armed Forces should be able to undertake a single large-scale operation like Operation TELIC (with a division-sized land component) while still maintaining a commitment to a small-scale operation in addition to the Standing Tasks and Commitments. To do more than this would require a significant increase in the size of the Armed Forces. These planning assumptions guide development of capability and are not intended to constrain or precisely describe the actual pattern of operational commitments. We may do less or may be able to do more. A period of recuperation is required after any operation to ensure that personnel can be rested and trained for other tasks, stockpiles can be replenished, and equipment replaced.

We are pleased to learn that according to *Lessons for the Future*, MOD intends to review the generation of force elements at readiness and the implications for notice to move times. But we feel that MOD should be more explicit in articulating what scale of forces can be offered for expeditionary operations of choice in the future, while ensuring adequate resources, equipment and training time. (Paragraph 75).

22. Force Elements at Readiness (FE@R) are regularly reviewed as part of the Short Term Plan process and in line with changes to the policy framework described in Defence Strategic Guidance. The FE@ R requirement is then published in the confidential section of the Departmental Plan, which forms the baseline for setting resource priorities. Defence Planning Assumptions are currently being reviewed as part of the revised guidance that will be published in 2005. This includes a more fundamental look at readiness in order to align timelines more closely with resources.

Command and Control

The appointment of a deployed UK National Contingent Commander worked effectively in Operation TELIC. (Paragraph 82).

23. We agree that the deployed UK national Contingent Commander based in the NCC headquarters worked effectively during Operation TELIC. We will keep under review what might be the best arrangements for any given operation.

We expect MOD to revisit the question of the deployability of PJHQ, raised in the SDR, in the light of recent operations, and we look forward to their conclusions. (Paragraph 82).

24. Through the Joint Force Headquarters, PJHQ is already deployable.

Command Relations with the Americans

We recommend that MOD considers whether the highest levels of British command structures might be made more adaptable so as to be able to operate more closely in parallel with their American counterparts, when UK and US forces are operating together. (Paragraph 84).

25. We do not agree. The Coalition command structures were closely integrated.

The Maritime Component

The Royal Fleet Auxiliary (RFA) made a vital contribution to the operation. MOD should ensure that the shortcomings which were highlighted are addressed. (Paragraph 88).

26. The Royal Navy is looking at the issue of Maritime Force Protection in the light of the lessons from Operation TELIC and the terrorist threat. The RFA will be included within this package. Measures range from individual body armour and night vision equipment to the Block Phalanx weapon system. These measures incur a cost and will be considered in relation to other priorities.

27. All RFA ships are currently fitted with close range weapons for self-defence. These weapons are either 20mm or 30mm cannon and 7.62 General Purpose Machine Guns. FORT VICTORIA and FORT GEORGE are also fitted with a Phalanx Close In Weapon System. All RFA crews are trained to operate and maintain the weapons onboard. Additional defensive measures are being considered to counter the asymmetric threat.

28. The replenishment capability of RFA ships varies between the different classes and depends on their specific roles. The larger FORT class ships are designed for full Task Force operations and are capable of conducting simultaneous multi-ship replenishment and flight deck operations. Others, such as the older LEAF class, only have a single ship replenishment capability. MOD is currently looking at the requirements for replacing the older RFA ships and that work will include analysis of the replenishment capability requirements for future ships.

Targeting

There is clear evidence of UK influence on the air targeting operations of the Coalition. Principally this influence seems to have been applied to issues of perception, specifically how attacking particular targets would be received by European allies. The extent to which the UK persuaded the US out of attacking certain targets on grounds of principle is less clear. We asked MOD for specific examples of UK influence but they failed to provide any, even on a classified basis. (Paragraph 98).

29. We note that the Committee recognises that the UK had influence in the decision-making process for Coalition targeting.

30. We are sorry the Committee has stated that we failed to provide them with examples of UK influence. We provided the Committee with classified material at the time of the request that we feel adequately answered their query. The Committee did not indicate at the time that they were dissatisfied.

We feel that the shortcomings in the practice and training of close air support by the RAF and land forces which have emerged in recent operations must be urgently addressed. This will require a reassessment of the numbers of and equipment for Forward Air Controllers, both on the ground and in the air, the provision of adequate targeting pods for individual aircraft and significantly greater exercising of these capabilities in a joint environment. Such exercises are likely to have to take place overseas since, as we understand it, no UK based facility exists for such training. (Paragraph 104).

31. The interface between the air and land environments is the subject of the Coningham/Keyes study. This is a joint initiative between LAND and STRIKE Commands. Training for Forward Air Controllers and Tactical Air Control Parties (TACP) is a specific study area and emerging findings are looking to realign exercises between the two commands in order to improve training opportunities. The Army has also created additional TACPs in each Division and is working to establish further teams in each manoeuvre Brigade. A programme to provide tactical satellite communications for these parties is scheduled to deliver by January 2005. The RAF acknowledge the need for more targeting pods but this is subject to the priorities placed on the Equipment Programme and has been judged unaffordable at this time.

32. We are considering proposals for an enhanced exercise programme.

Effective and timely arrangements for assessing battle damage are crucial for continuously informing the campaign plan and for establishing whether the aim of minimising damage to civilians and civilian infrastructure has been achieved. We look to MOD to exploit the latest technological advances to further improve the speed and accuracy of battle damage assessment. (Paragraph 106).

33. We agree that timely Battle Damage Assessment (BDA) is important. During Operation TELIC, however, the scale of the air campaign meant there were insufficient resources available to carry out the BDA task during major combat operations. Technical and intelligence availability issues continue to limit our ability to conduct BDA as effectively as we would wish; future developments of Unmanned Aerial Vehicles (UAVs) and Intelligence, Surveillance, Target Acquisition and Reconnaissance (ISTAR) platforms may alleviate this.

Use of Reserves

Call-out and mobilisation

While we are pleased to learn that for Operations TELIC 2 and 3, MOD has been able to give most reservists 21 days notice to report, we are concerned that for TELIC 1 reservists were given 14 days notice to report, and in some cases considerably less. We expect MOD to ensure that the appropriate lessons are learned to avoid the need for such short notice to report, and to recognise the impact of this on reservists, their families and their employers. (Paragraph 116).

34. Notice to report for compulsory call-out is set by operational requirements. Ideally we would aim to give both regular reservists and volunteer reservists 21 days notice to report for service, but this cannot always be achieved. For TELIC I, in order to ensure the reserves were ready in time, generally we were only able to give 14 days notice to report. In some instances notice to report was considerably shorter. For operational reasons we were unable to avoid mobilising a number of key enablers soon after the call-out order was made.

35. For TELIC II and III, in general we were able to give reservists 21 days notice to report. Again, this could not be guaranteed and a small number of reservists received a shorter notice to report due mainly to late changes to operational requirements.

36. As the Operation matures and planning can be carried out further in advance, we hope to move to 30 days notice to report for Op TELIC. In practice for TELIC IV we have generally achieved over 28 days notice to report and we shall strive to maintain this level of notice. However, it must be understood that there will always be last minute changes of requirement and/or operational circumstances which mean that we cannot guarantee a set notice to report period for reservists.

We expect MOD and the reserve organisations to take appropriate action to ensure that reservists are made fully aware of their liability for call out. (Paragraph 117).

37. Every individual joining the Volunteer Reserve is made aware of his or her call-out liability under the Reserve Forces Act 1996. In addition, when joining the Regular Armed Forces, individuals are informed that they may have a Regular Reserve liability when they complete their term of regular service. They are also reminded of this liability when they are discharged from service and their Regular Reserve liability commences.

38. During the initial stages of the Op TELIC Lessons Identified exercise, however, it became clear that many reservists were unsure of the extent of their call-out liability and that they were unprepared for mobilisation. As a direct result of this finding all three Services have instigated 'Mobilisation Matters' training packages which are being given to Volunteer Reservists as part of their routine training.

We recommend that MOD consider what action can be taken to ensure that the substantial proportion of regular reservists who failed their medicals return to being 'fit for role'. (Paragraph 119).

39. There are established procedures for monitoring the fitness of Volunteer Reservists who fail mobilisation medicals. For Regular Reservists, however, there are no procedures to monitor medical fitness, nor is there any way of enforcing the maintenance of medical fitness once an individual has left the Regular Forces. As part of the Lessons Identified process, however, we are considering the future role of the Regular Reserve. This will include considering methods of monitoring and maintaining medical fitness and dental health. At the time of writing it is too early to say what conclusions may be reached.

Overall, it appears that the majority of reservists mobilising through Chilwell considered that they had received adequate training before being deployed. However, we are concerned about the non-alignment of Territorial Army (TA) and Regular shooting standards and expect MOD to address this issue as soon as possible. (Paragraph 122).

40. The TA has a limited number of training days per year compared to the training available to Regular soldiers. It must, therefore, be recognised that we cannot expect the TA to match Regular soldiers' training standards in all subjects including Skill at Arms. Nevertheless, previous to Operation TELIC, Skill at Arms was one of many areas where we delivered improvements by introducing Phase One Training: the Common Military Syllabus (Recruit) TA (on 1 April 2003). This programme not only reduces the training gap with Regular soldiers across a range of skills but also identifies that training which needs to be addressed on mobilisation. Skill at Arms is one of the basic training requirements for all soldiers and is under continuous development. Concurrent activity across a number of work strands for the TA seeks to improve both the annual Skill at Arms standard and attainment level required for the TA's emerging roles.

41. In addition, once called-out, members of the TA undergo a short period of pre-deployment training. The aim of this training is to prepare reservists for the theatre to which they will deploy and provide refresher training in key areas including weapons handling. Once this training is complete, reservists are deployed to theatre. On arrival, they then undergo further training to ensure that they are fully prepared for the role they are to perform.

Finance and compensation issues

We are concerned to learn that some TA reservists experienced problems regarding their pay. We understand that for future operations, where significant numbers of reservists are deployed, PJHQ have agreed to the deployment of a Reserves Cell whose role will include issues such as pay and allowances. We expect MOD to ensure that this lesson is implemented in full. (Paragraph 125).

42. We accept that there were a few problems with pay delivery. Some reservists' pay statements did not get delivered to units in the desert. This meant that they did not know that they were being paid, or how much they were being paid. For the small number that did experience pay delivery problems, we are not aware of any delay in the payment of reservists' basic military salary. However, there have been some late payments of allowances for reservists during Operation TELIC, which are attributable to delays in the administrative process for taking the reservist on strength at the Theatre unit. In addition, there have also been delays in handling claims for financial assistance. This is due, in the

main, to reservists failing to provide the evidence necessary to process claims. Both of these issues were identified during the Operation TELIC lessons identified process and action is in hand to improve the administrative systems in use.

43. We fully accept the Committee's recommendation. A dedicated Reserves Cell that can deal with reserve issues, including pay, has been in theatre since TELIC. The need for such a cell has been written into our future deployment plans.

It is clearly wrong that reservists who are compulsorily mobilised for combat operations should lose out financially. We note that to date only a small number of appeals have been made by reservists dissatisfied with their individual financial arrangements. We recommend that these be considered sympathetically and that MOD monitor closely the numbers and outcomes of such appeals over the coming months. (Paragraph 126).

44. The Committee appears to have misunderstood the Financial Assistance process. Should a reservist be dissatisfied with the amount of financial assistance awarded by MOD, they have a right to appeal to an <u>independent</u> Reserve Forces Appeals Tribunal. This is organised by the Employment Tribunal Service who supply the members of the Appeals Tribunal. As the appeal procedure is independent of MOD, we cannot influence the outcome of appeals. However, we do make every effort to resolve cases sympathetically before an appeal hearing is needed.

45. At the time of writing the total number of appeals that had been submitted was 116 of which five were reservist financial appeals. Two were resolved to the reservists' satisfaction before the appeal date, leaving three which have gone to appeal. The Tribunal found in favour of MOD in two cases. The final case is still outstanding.

We expect MOD to ensure that the procedures for reservists claiming financial assistance are streamlined and less intrusive. (Paragraph 127).

46. We agree with the Committee's recommendation. As already detailed in the recent Defence White Paper, work is in hand to produce new regulations governing the award of both Reservist Standard Award and Reservists Hardship Award. The new regulations will take into account the lessons arising from the mobilisation for Iraq. This work is being undertaken as a priority.

Employment issues

We note that MOD has commissioned a study to measure the degree of employer support for the mobilisation of the Reserve and look forward to seeing the findings and the lessons that MOD identify. But we consider that MOD needs to adopt a more proactive approach to identifying cases where reservists have experienced employment problems following a period of mobilisation. Reservists need to be assured that they will not lose their jobs, as a result of being mobilised, and that support will be available if they encounter such problems. (Paragraph 129).

47. We agree that a proactive approach is the best way of dealing with this problem. That is why, in cooperation with the regional Reserve Forces and Cadets Associations, we have introduced regional Employer Support Executives to liaise with employers on a number of

issues including employment problems following mobilisation. We are also introducing Unit Employer Support Officers to strengthen our capability in this area further.

48. We do not take the support of employers for granted and have, for many years, run a campaign to win and maintain the support of employers for the Reserve Forces. Support to British Reserve Employers provides the main elements of this campaign. Since the beginning of Op TELIC we have been writing to the employers of those reservists who have been called out to thank them for their support. Additionally, we have held a number of regional receptions in order to thank employers personally.

49. With regard to employment protection, under the Reserve Forces (Safeguard of Employment) Act 1985, employers are required to take back into employment former employees who have completed called-out service. The Act also deals with the terms and conditions of reservists when reinstated to civilian employment. If an employer fails to take a reservist back into employment or infringes any of his or her rights under the 1985 Act, the reservist may apply to a Reinstatement Committee which will decide on the matter. The Committee has the power to require employment to be made available to the reservist, or may order the employer to pay compensation, or both. Our experience so far is that there have been 17 cases that have been heard by Reinstatement Committees.

50. We are fully aware of the need to monitor reinstatement difficulties, and we liaise closely with the employment Tribunal Service to keep full track of all Reinstatement Committee hearings.

We are very concerned to learn that 11 members of the TA in Germany (over a quarter of the TA in Germany deployed to Operation TELIC), who form part of a key squadron (the Amphibious Engineer Squadron), lost their jobs with civilian employers on returning from deployment on Operation TELIC. We expect MOD and the reserve organisations to raise these matters with the relevant authorities within Germany and with the civilian employers of the TA reservists in Germany. (Paragraph 131).

51. We were very concerned to learn that 11 members of the TA in Germany lost their civilian jobs on returning from deployment on Operation TELIC. These individuals were not protected by the provisions of the Reserve Forces (Safeguard of Employment) Act 1985, as they are British nationals who live overseas and are not protected by UK law. We have, therefore, as a temporary measure offered all those who were unable to regain their civilian jobs Full-Time Reserve Service with the Army for 12 months or until they are able to find alternative work. In addition, we plan to raise the matter of reservists' employment protection with the relevant authorities within Germany.

We are concerned that the requirement on reservists to inform their employers of their reserve status seems to have been announced ahead of the findings of MOD's own study on employer support. There does not seem to have been prior consultation with members of the Reserve. We recommend that MOD set out why it chose to make this change at this time. (Paragraph 132).

52. This subject has been the topic of much debate both within MOD and with reservists and employers. Surveys undertaken by the Ministry of Defence have shown that a large majority of reservists have already told their employers that they are members of the

Volunteer Reserve. In addition, when reservists are mobilised their employers are automatically informed of their membership of the reserve forces. Therefore, we do not expect routine employer notification to have a significant impact on employer support.

53. The introduction of employer notification was announced by Written Ministerial Statement on 3 February 2004 (Official Report, Column WS25). Currently members of the Volunteer Reserve Forces (VRF) are required to declare their employment status and to provide details of their employer(s) to MOD. They are also encouraged to inform their employer(s) of their membership of the VRF and of their liability for training and call out. A majority are believed to have done so. They will now be required to give their consent for MOD to do so automatically. This change of policy is a reasonable requirement for the individual. It will permit employers to plan for an employee's absence for full time military service and thereby contribute directly to reducing mobilisation risk by minimising the likelihood of employer applications for exemption at time of call out.

54. Employer notification was implemented with effect from 1 April 2004 for all new entrants to the VRF and for all current members of the VRF as they re-engage unless granted an exemption waiver. Employer notification will also apply with effect from 1 April 2005 to those who do not routinely re-engage such as commissioned officers.

Impact on the Reserves

It is unreasonable that reserve personnel deployed on Operation TELIC should have to do additional service, on top of the six to nine months taken up by that tour, to qualify for their annual bounty and we recommend that MOD waives this requirement. (Paragraph 134).

55. We disagree. Reservists do not earn training bounty when undertaking mobilised service. Although they are delivering operational capability by carrying out their trade tasks in an operational environment, they are not meeting the bounty requirements for training. The reason for this rule is that it is a *training* bounty, paid to those who undertake the required elements of peacetime training to ensure they are fit for mobilisation. We recognise, however, that mobilisation has made it difficult for some reservists to meet their training bounty requirement. Authority has therefore been granted for mobilised service to count in lieu of the continuous training element conducted during annual camp. Nevertheless, reservists must additionally complete their weekend training with their volunteer reserve unit in order to qualify for bounty.

MOD has identified a number of lessons relating to the Reserve from the experience of Operation TELIC. We look to MOD to implement these lessons in full. We welcome the announcement that, following Operation TELIC, MOD is adjusting the arrangements for the higher management of the Reserve and that the Directorate of Reserve Forces and Cadets will come under the direct command of the Vice Chief of the Defence Staff, which reflects the importance of this key part of our Armed Forces. (Paragraph 135).

56. We agree with the Committee that the reserves form a key part of the Armed Forces. In order to reflect this we have reviewed and amended our organisational structure to reflect

this. A new two star reserve post, Assistant Chief of Defence Staff (Reserves and Cadets), has been established who reports directly to Vice Chief of the Defence Staff.

57. With regard to the recommendations arising out of the use of reserves during Operation TELIC, many of these have already been implemented. Work continues to implement those that remain. In addition, we will continue to modify and improve our policies and practices on the use of Reserves in light of current and future operations.

Throughout our inquiry we have come into contact with a range of reservists who served on Operation TELIC. As with the Regular service personnel, we have been impressed with their dedication and the invaluable contribution they made. We concur with MOD's conclusion that reservists 'showed the highest quality and commitment… their value in all phases of an operation has again been demonstrated.' (Paragraph 136).

58. We agree. We are grateful for the commitment and professionalism with which reservists carry out their duties.

Defence Medical Services

Manning

We find it worrying that some five years after the Strategic Defence Review the problems in the Defence Medical Services (DMS), in particular the problem of under-manning, appear to be as bad as they ever have been. We were alarmed to learn that for the major specialities for war MOD had 'emptied the boxes' for Operation TELIC. Further deployments in the near future are only likely to exacerbate the problems. (Paragraph 143).

59. It is simply not true that "some five years after the Strategic Defence the problems in the DMS" are "as bad as they ever were". Compared with March 1999, in January 2004 we had nearly 350 more fully trained medical personnel, and over 500 more trainees in the pipeline.

60. We are making good progress in addressing shortages in those areas where under-manning remains a problem, with an emphasis on certain key clinical specialties: A&E, Anaesthetics, General Medicine, General Surgery, Orthopaedics, Burns and Plastics and Radiology.

61. The Medical Manning and Retention Review has established a new pay structure to improve comparability with the NHS, and the flexibility to respond to future NHS changes. Pay for our Medical and Dental Officers improved by 10 per cent last year. We have introduced a system of financial recruitment initiatives (the "Golden Hellos" scheme) targeting certain categories of consultants, General Medical Practitioners and certain categories of nurses.

62. Other measures to address under-manning include greater integration of the medical reserve and the use of civilian medical personnel on enduring operations. One civilian consultant anaesthetist has been working in Bosnia since December 03. We also intend to send a civilian consultant team to Iraq.

63. Operation TELIC was a large-scale operation; the most demanding one-off deployment for which we plan. Unsurprisingly, the DMS, in common with other components of our Armed Forces, was fully occupied supporting this commitment. But as with all previous operations, we were fully able to meet the operational requirement.

64. We continue to provide essential medical force protection to the UK Armed Forces in Iraq. We remain confident of our continuing ability to meet the MOD's planning assumptions, and hence to support likely future deployments.

We acknowledge that the manning issue is not an easy one to address quickly, but we look to MOD, the Department of Health, the NHS and the medical profession to support the DMS in its efforts to find new and innovative solutions. (Paragraph 144).

65. We are already working closely with the Department of Health and the NHS. Under the terms of a Concordat signed with the Department of Health in September 2002, we have established a Partnership Board to address matters of mutual interest. The Partnership Board also includes representatives from the NHS and the devolved administrations in Scotland, Northern Ireland and Wales.

66. A current initiative is to deploy NHS Integrated Medical Teams to assist in the provision of medical support on enduring operations. This will release regular and reserve medical specialists for short notice operations, and alleviate deployment fatigue. It will also provide career development and vocational training for NHS staff in a challenging environment.

67. We have already received positive responses from four NHS Trusts, and hope to deploy the first medical specialists from a NHS acute trust in January 2005. We anticipate that, if this deployment is successful, it will lead to further positive responses from other NHS Trusts.

We recommend that MOD bring together the Department of Health, the NHS and the medical profession with the DMS in order urgently to identify solutions to the problem of increasing specialism among surgeons in the NHS. (Paragraph 146).

68. We are already engaged with the Department of Health, the NHS and the medical profession on these issues, and we are making good progress.

69. We are confident that we will be able to make the increasing trend towards specialisation among surgeons in the NHS work for us, rather than against us.

70. Our surgeons must train to NHS standards and expectations, and must, therefore, have a sub-speciality that benefits their NHS Trust. Equally, our surgeons need to retain competencies of a general nature for use on deployment. The two requirements are not necessarily opposed, as most sub-specialities will involve transferable skills.

71. We are working to ensure that, where necessary, we can provide our surgeons with the additional training they require to meet operational demands. For example, we have an arrangement with South Africa whereby DMS surgeons receive specialist trauma training there. This training is vital to the DMS as it enables surgeons to train in the treatment of gunshot wounds.

We are most concerned to learn that 47 medical reservists have resigned on returning from Operation TELIC, and that MOD is aware of further resignations from Army medical reservists. The number of resignations represents some six per cent of the 760 medical reservists deployed. We expect MOD to monitor this issue closely, to identify the reasons behind the resignations, and to take account of these in its recruitment and retention efforts. (Paragraph 147).

72. Every year a small number of our medical reservists leave for a variety of reasons, including an unwillingness to participate in future operations following exposure to the realities of a challenging deployment. This is to be expected, and we would certainly not wish to retain reservists who have become either unable or unwilling to meet their obligations.

73. So far, the numbers of medical reservists leaving, for whatever reason, following Operation TELIC are not exceptional by comparison with previous years.

74. If anything, the departure rate for medical reservists compares favourably with the normal average annual turnover rate for reservists as a whole. However, as with all retention issues the MOD will keep this under constant review.

Impact on the NHS

This was the first operation where all the medical personnel deployed came almost exclusively from the NHS and it appears that the arrangements, such as the liaison between MOD, the Department of Health, and NHS Trusts worked well. However, thankfully, the number of casualties was low and the arrangements for treating casualties in NHS hospitals were not fully tested. (Paragraph 149).

75. We welcome the Select Committees' acknowledgement of the success of our liaison with the Department of Health and NHS Trusts.

Medical equipment and supplies

We are pleased to learn that lessons about the need to have more medical supplies on the shelves rather than over-relying on UORs have been recognised. We expect MOD to identify the appropriate balance between holding items and relying on UORs. We also expect MOD to review any cases from Operation TELIC where inadequate or insufficient equipment may have disadvantaged clinical outcomes and, if any such cases are identified, to take appropriate action to avoid such situations occurring in the future. (Paragraph 152).

76. We are working hard with the Medical Supplies Agency and the Defence Logistics Organisation to establish and maintain an appropriate balance between holding items and relying on UORs.

77. We are not aware of any cases where inadequate or insufficient equipment disadvantaged clinical outcomes. Allegations to the contrary have not been substantiated.

Deployment

Sea Lift and Air Lift

We conclude that deploying such a large force to the Gulf in the time available was a significant achievement. (Paragraph 155).

78. We strongly agree that deploying such a large force to the Gulf in the time available was a significant achievement and a credit to our logistics organisation.

MOD should identify how the challenges of limited landing slots for aircraft and small seaports could be addressed in the future. (Paragraph 158).

79. We note the committee's recommendation, although the committee has also recognised that we were successful in deploying a large force to the Gulf in a short period of time. It will clearly be important that the planning for any deployment takes account of the physical constraints at the points of disembarkation.

We recognise the achievement of the DTMA in securing the sea lift for Operation TELIC. We recommend that, drawing on the experience from Operation TELIC, MOD should undertake a review of ro-ro shipping to inform its future planning. (Paragraph 162).

80. We agree that the acquisition of sufficient sealift was a major achievement and vindicated our procedures and practices. The availability of RoRo shipping is reviewed by the Department on a continuous basis, which will inform future planning.

The action taken by MOD ensured that the UK had sufficient lift, but the outcome could well have been different. For any future operations, MOD needs to avoid competing directly with the US for outsize lift and co-ordinate its efforts to secure such assets. (Paragraph 163).

81. Every effort is made as part of the planning process to avoid competing with our allies for outsize lift.

Recent operations have highlighted the need for sufficient sea and air lift. We look to MOD to ensure that those assets that have performed their task well are available to our Armed Forces in the future. We regret that the A400M programme, which is intended to meet the UK's Future Transport Aircraft requirement, has experienced delays to its planned in-service date. We expect MOD to ensure that the current forecast in-service date is met and that any capability gaps from delays already experienced are filled. (Paragraph 167).

82. The Department is procuring 25 A400M not 180 aircraft (which is the total number of aircraft being purchased through OCCAR) as mentioned in the report at paragraph 166. The Out-of-Service Date for the Hercules C-130K fleet is linked to the In-Service Date (ISD) of the A400M. We expect the current A400M ISD to be met, but if for any reason this does not happen, then Hercules and C-17 aircraft will fill any capability gaps.

Urgent Operational Requirements

We acknowledge that there were constraints on when the UOR process could begin, but it is of real concern that in some cases this resulted in Armed Forces personnel not having access to the full complement of equipment, such as Minimi machine guns and Underslung Grenade Launchers. (Paragraph 177).

83. The Department accepts that, on occasion, Urgent Operational Requirements' (UOR) delivery timescales will be tight. Any shortfalls that occurred did not in the event affect operational capability. The decision as to whether our forces were ready for combat operations, quite rightly, rested with the operational commanders. They would not have allowed their troops to cross the line without the necessary equipment for the task.

Much of the equipment procured as UORs made a significant contribution to the success of the campaign and, in most cases, industry supplied equipment at very short notice. However UORs are not the solution in every case. MOD needs to be better informed of which types of equipment and capabilities can be delivered in UOR timescales—there were a number of cases where equipment was not delivered by the time required or where users did not have a full complement. We do not consider that MOD planning properly recognised that the delivery date for a piece of equipment and the date by which a capability is achieved are not the same. If personnel are to be confident and fully efficient with their equipment there must be adequate time for familiarisation, training and integration. Furthermore, given the desire stated in the recent White Paper to be able to intervene anywhere in the world at short notice, we believe that the risks of relying on UORs instead of holding adequate stocks, are not sufficiently well analysed or understood in MOD's risk assessment processes. (Paragraph 181).

84. The right balance needs to be struck between having expensive stocks on the shelves and relying on procurement during the readiness period. To keep large stock levels—so that we could do another operation of this size at shorter notice—would be very costly. We have to factor affordability into the equation, and make judgements on the likelihood of action being required. The Defence Logistics Organisation (DLO) holds stocks in accordance with agreed planning assumptions. These assumptions have recently been looked at in detail and were reissued in revised form in August 2003. We have started to identify the detailed actions we need to take regarding stock levels.

85. The UOR process is used to fine-tune military capability to ensure UK forces are as well equipped as possible for the tasks they are asked to carry out. There will always be capabilities we would like to have, but which we will not be able to obtain in time for operations. But it must be borne in mind that the capability we do have is highly potent, and with relatively minor enhancement provides a strong basis on which to build successful operations, such as those so recently carried out.

86. While the Department acknowledges that tight delivery timescales can reduce the time available for training prior to commencement of operations, many UORs were procured to provide additional equipment of a type already held or to make minor modifications to it. Such measures do not need much extra training. Moreover, the help provided by the

deployment of both the Armoured Training Development Unit and Infantry Training Development Unit into theatre was invaluable.

There are likely to be positive lessons from the UOR process which have applicability to MOD's normal equipment acquisition processes: for example, where UORs were used to accelerate existing programmes. We expect MOD to identify and implement these and reflect on the appropriateness of UOR procurement becoming institutionalised. (Paragraph 183).

87. There is a clear process in the Department for capturing Lessons Identified from Operations and exercises and the same applies to the UOR process. In addition, the National Audit Office (NAO) is in the middle of a study of the Department's UOR process to see if it is the most effective/efficient way of meeting urgent military needs. A report is expected during the summer.

We expect MOD to evaluate fully the performance of the equipment procured as UORs and the specific enhancements they provided to the UK's military capabilities. This evaluation must also take full account of the views of those members of the Armed Forces who used the equipment in action. Disposing of useful equipment cannot represent good value for money if it then has to be reacquired in the future. (Paragraph 184).

88. The Department assesses whether we should retain UORs in-service after an operation, and whether we can extend the enhancements across equipment fleets. If an enhancement is retained, our analysis will usually have shown that the benefit it offers in improved performance outweighs the possible complications in sustainability.

89. The UOR process allows us to respond to operations in extreme environments (such as the desert) and to the specific capabilities we anticipate opponents to have. We could not afford to equip all our forces against every threat and climatic extreme: a sensible balance has to be struck. At the conclusion of operations we review whether we should resource the continuation of individual UORs in-service from the Defence budget. We have been doing this recently for Operation TELIC UORs as part of the planning round.

90. The Department acknowledges the Committee's point that it can be wasteful to sell UORs and then buy them back. But we must be realistic about resource constraints: we cannot always afford to retain all the UOR equipment we want. In many cases we may not keep equipment in-service if it has been used heavily, or if technology is moving very fast. It may be better to buy state-of-the-art equipment rather than keep kit in warehouses for years.

The Start of Operations

From planning to operations—what was found

The Committee congratulates the Royal Navy for the success of the complex and demanding operation to clear mines from the waterway to Umm Qasr and urges the MOD to review, as a matter of urgency, the capability of the Royal Navy to undertake mine clearance operations in shallow and very shallow waters, given the likely need for increasing amphibious operations in the littoral. (Paragraph 195).

91. In the light of our experiences during Operation TELIC, we are incrementally improving our ability to conduct Mine Counter-Measure (MCM) operations in shallow and very shallow water. We have already established the Fleet Unmanned Underwater Vehicle Unit (FUUVU) with an interim capability. It completed training in January 2004 and has deployed operationally to Iraq in support of the Iraq Survey Group.

92. Building on the work done by the FUUVU, we will over the next five years, roll out a Mid-Term MCM Coherency package that will introduce additional Unmanned Underwater Vehicles (UUVs) into the Fleet, upgrade the command systems in the SANDOWN Minehunter and provide an improved Network Enabled Capability that will enable information to be shared electronically between ships and other Fleet units. These enhancements will improve significantly our current capability to undertake mine clearance in shallow and very shallow water. In the longer term we are developing a Future Mine-Countermeasures Capability that will:

- Further improve our ability to conduct operations in very shallow water (2m - 10m),

- Facilitate the greater exploitation of Unmanned Underwater Vehicles and remote MCM concepts, and

- Provide a more developed Network-Enabled Capability to the MCM Commander and improved frontline support to MCM units.

The approach to Basra

The operation to take Basra was a significant military achievement. One measure of its success—and in the context of an effects-based operation an important one—was that just one week later there were joint UK/Iraqi patrols. (Paragraph 202).

93. We agree that the operation to take Basra by UK forces was a significant military achievement. Their subsequent performance since that time, including both the mounting of joint UK/Iraqi patrols and their extensive training, mentoring and monitoring of the Iraqi security forces, has again demonstrated their professionalism and versatility.

Major Defence Equipment

Overall Performance

We are pleased to learn that in most cases the major defence equipments performed well in the difficult conditions encountered in Iraq although, given the nature of the enemy, many equipments were not tested to the full. (Paragraph 209).

94. The Department agrees that most of our defence equipment performed well in the challenging environmental conditions in Iraq. Although the Iraqis did not make the best use of their capabilities, that is something for which Coalition forces can take credit. The campaign plan was designed to overwhelm the regime, present it with a multiplicity of problems and disrupt its command and control capabilities. Clearly we were successful in this aim.

Availability of Equipment

The availability of most defence equipment was generally high during Operation TELIC. However, it is disappointing that an impressive capability such as HMS Ocean is let down by unreliable landing craft and 'that there are difficulties with the acceptance of the new landing craft.' We expect MOD to remedy this issue as soon as possible to ensure that the capabilities of HMS Ocean are maximised. (Paragraph 213).

95. The full complement of four landing craft (MK 5A LCVP) embarked from HMS OCEAN during Operation TELIC. Although problems were encountered with control of hydraulic and salt water cooling systems, work is now in hand to rectify these faults. The MK 5A LCVP Landing Craft is being replaced by the MK 5B craft. Whilst there were delays in the early stages of the build programme the total order of 16 craft was delivered and accepted into service on schedule (March 04).

Communication and Information Systems

It concerns us that for the next four to five years we will continue to be dependent upon Skynet 4 which has recognised limitations and which let us down on this occasion. (Paragraph 215).

96. It is not the case that Skynet 4 services will continue unchanged until replaced by a new Skynet 5 constellation of satellites in four or five years' time. The Skynet 5 service provider (Paradigm Communications Services) took ownership and operational management of Skynet 4 space and ground assets in mid 2003 and is already introducing improved services. By early 2005 we expect to have a full Skynet 5 service operating over the existing Skynet 4 satellites and expect from around 2007 the service provider to be introducing new satellites.

97. Both current and planned satellite communications capability use military (Skynet) and commercial satellite communications as they offer different benefits according to the circumstances. The diversity that is offered by this approach has proved useful. One of the Skynet satellites did experience a problem briefly during the operation but the majority of communications traffic was transferred to other available satellites.

Operation TELIC highlighted serious shortcomings in the reliability, capacity and redundancy of the UK's communications and information systems, which to a large extent are a consequence of under-investment in the past. While we acknowledge that work is in hand to address these shortcomings, we find it very worrying that it will be some time before any real improvements will be seen, particularly given the frequency with which UK Armed Forces are now involved in operations, and the increased need to communicate effectively not only within UK forces but also with our allies. (Paragraph 218).

98. The communications links used during operations in Iraq were carried over a diverse range of military and commercial satellite bearer systems. Additional capacity was available had it been needed. The total data bandwidth used during the operation exceeded that deployed for any previous overseas operation.

99. Difficulties lay not so much with the systems themselves but the gateways and interfaces between them. As explained in Lessons for the Future, some of these could not always cope with the volume of traffic. We are aware of the problems inherent in operating a variety of different communications systems and are developing the capability to manage our way round the inevitable difficulties encountered.

100. As well as improvements to satellite communications through the Skynet 5 programme, other communication infrastructure improvements will begin to come on stream from 2004. The achievement of In-Service Date (ISD) for the BOWMAN tactical radio system (ahead of target) was announced in March 2004 and the CORMORANT theatre system for connecting deployed headquarters is also due to come into service later this year. Both these systems have been developed for interoperability with the US and other allies as a key consideration by, for example, incorporating NATO standards.

Combat Identification

We welcome the overall finding of the National Audit Office that on Operation TELIC, the measures, procedures and training relating to combat identification were largely effective. We are disappointed that a copy of the review of combat identification undertaken by the Vice Chief of Defence Staff, which was provided to the National Audit Office, was not made available to the Defence Committee during its inquiry. (Paragraph 222).

101. We note the Committee's comments.

We expect MOD to make available to Parliament and the Committee the summaries of the conclusions of the reports of the Boards of Inquiry into individual blue on blue incidents as soon as possible and for the summaries to provide sufficient information on the causes of the incidents and the lessons learned in order to reassure the Armed Forces and ourselves that everything practicable was done to minimise the possibility of such incidents. (Paragraph 229).

102. We note the Committee's comments. We have indicated to Parliament that summaries of the conclusions of the Board of Inquiry reports will be made available to the Library of the House, but only when all other related proceedings are entirely complete.

We expect MOD to implement the lessons from Operation TELIC relating to combat identification. MOD should push forward with the work with its allies to agree on a single system. The latter is particularly important given that future UK military action is most likely to be as part of a Coalition. We note MOD's view that the opportunities for fratricide in an increasingly complex battle space are likely to increase, but look to MOD to identify the required action and make the necessary investment to ensure that such incidents are reduced to a minimum. (Paragraph 233).

103. The Department remains committed to improving combat effectiveness and minimising all casualties by improving Combat Identification among other measures. This will also minimise the risk of fratricide. Lessons identified from cases of fratricide during operations in Iraq will inform all three elements of Combat ID capability - situational awareness, target identification and tactics, techniques and procedures. We continue to

work with allies on a range of Combat ID issues, including efforts to introduce an interoperable target identification system for the ground environment.

UAVS

We are pleased to hear that, despite its chequered past, Phoenix made a valuable contribution to the operation. We support the robust approach being adopted in relation to the Watchkeeper UAV programme, which aims to 'nail the…requirement and to make sure that the companies deliver that which we have asked for' although we continue to be concerned that the accelerated in-service date for the programme may not be met. We will continue to monitor the progress of this key programme. (Paragraph 236).

104. The Department notes the Committee's concerns about the accelerated in-service date of WATCHKEEPER. Two proposals for the demonstration and manufacture phase were received in March 2004 and are being assessed. The main investment decision is due later in 2004 at which time a formal in-service date will be set.

We consider it well worthwhile that MOD is assessing the usefulness of manportable UAVs for current operations in Iraq. We expect MOD to reflect the results of this assessment when deciding on the overall mix of UAVs for the future. (Paragraph 237).

105. Experience from the deployment of the Desert Hawk man-portable UAVs in Iraq and from the work conducted under the Joint UAV Experimental Programme (JUEP) will be taken into account in informing decisions about meeting Intelligence, Surveillance, Target Acquisition and Reconnaissance (ISTAR) capability requirements in the future.

Apache

We conclude that there are key lessons from the United States' experience in Iraq which MOD needs to take into account when developing its tactics, techniques and procedures for its Apache helicopters. We expect MOD to take the required action to ensure that UK Apache helicopters are as capable as they can be, given the new sorts of environments and operations they are likely to be operating in. (Paragraph 240).

106. The UK has developed close links with the US in the development of the concepts for employing AH. The US lessons from their experiences in Iraq validate much of what is already laid down in the UK doctrine for Air Manoeuvre. The US did experience problems during certain missions in Iraq and the lessons in terms of mission planning, all-arms employment and threat assessment have been incorporated.

107. In sum, the positive and negative aspects of the Apache helicopter's experience on Operation TELIC have been examined and the lessons learnt will be included in tactics, techniques and procedures.

Sea King

The Sea King helicopter made a significant contribution to the operation and highlighted the benefit of acquiring equipment that is sufficiently adaptable. However, we are concerned to learn that, at times, the Sea King provided the only dedicated stand-off sensor coverage for 3 Commando Brigade's operations on the Al Faw peninsula. We expect MOD to ensure that the Astor programme meets its in-service date to fill the current capability gap. (Paragraph 241).

108. The ASTOR programme is on track to meet its approved In-Service Date of autumn 2005, with Full Operating Capability due to be achieved by 2008.

We expect MOD to ensure that the lessons identified to minimise the Sea King's vulnerability are fully implemented. (Paragraph 242).

109. All potential vulnerabilities of maritime helicopters are naturally kept under constant review. The Royal Navy proactively manages risk. With the exception of Sea King Mk4 (Commando) helicopters, no maritime helicopters are currently fitted with either Defensive Aids Suites (DAS), or armoured seating for the crew. The fitting of DAS has been an aspiration for some time, and its potential benefits have been highlighted again in Operation TELIC; but it had not previously achieved a sufficiently high resourcing priority within the Equipment Programme (EP). The priority list for the fitting of DAS is assessed to be Lynx HMA Mk 3/8, followed by Sea King Mk 7 ASAC and Merlin HM Mk 1. In EP 04, a funding measure to equip a number of Lynx with DAS has been successful, and 12 sets will be funded. This should provide additional protection to those Lynx when deployed on operational tasking from 2005. Until upgrade programmes are approved for the remaining aircraft types, protection will be achieved through operating procedures and tactics designed to minimise risk.

The Defence White Paper

We have announced our intention to undertake an inquiry into the Defence White Paper. We will also continue to monitor the progress of the Future Rapid Effects System (FRES) programme as part of our annual inquiry into defence procurement. (Paragraph 246).

110. We welcome the Committee's inquiry into the Defence White Paper. It is also appropriate to monitor the progress of the FRES programme, which will be an important part of the delivery of a medium weight land force.

Personal Equipment and Protection

We are pleased to note that, following its initial rejection of the concerns about personal equipment and protection, MOD now acknowledges that there was a problem which had a detrimental impact on service personnel. Robust arrangements should now be introduced to gauge the views of more junior ranks and specialists whose widespread concerns do not seem to be properly understood, reflected and acted upon by more senior commanders and officials further up the chain. (Paragraph 249).

111. The Department has fully acknowledged that there were shortages of certain items of personal equipment. However, sufficient stocks of desert clothing, ECBA, NBC equipment etc. were procured to meet the stated operational requirements. The key difficulty was our inability to track assets once they were delivered to theatre. Arrangements already exist to gauge junior ranks' views on issues of concern to them via the chain of command.

Desert Boots and Clothing

The issue of the availability of desert clothing and boots during Operation TELIC has been both a confusing and worrying story. MOD should clarify its position on the circumstances in which desert clothing and boots are to be used and ensure that all service personnel understand the position. MOD clearly underestimated the impact on morale of failing to provide service personnel with the clothing and boots which they required and expected. We find it unacceptable that some two weeks after the start of the combat phase 60 per cent of the additional clothing requirement that had been ordered was not available in theatre. We understand that MOD has now increased its stockholding of desert and tropical clothing and boots up to a total of 32,000 sets. We expect MOD to keep the level of stockholding under review. (Paragraph 257)."

112. Sufficient stocks of desert clothing and desert boots were ordered to meet the stated operational requirements. However, the Department acknowledges that some personnel experienced shortages. In light of operations in Iraq, the policy has been reviewed and stockholdings have been increased to cater for 32,000 personnel.

113. The MOD is confident that arrangements for ensuring personnel and units understand when Desert Clothing and Boots are to be used are sufficiently robust.

Enhanced Body Armour

Body armour is another example of where MOD's in-theatre distribution and tracking led to shortages in critical equipment. MOD should identify and implement solutions to address these shortcomings and ensure that service personnel receive the equipment they are entitled to. (Paragraph 262).

114. Measures have been introduced in the STP/EP 04 programme to provide incremental improvements to logistic tracking and visibility. In the short term, efforts have focused upon enhancements to the Consignment Visibility system and retention of the Total Asset Visibility system procured as a UOR measure for Operation TELIC. Funding has also been agreed for the equipment programme to develop Management of the Joint Deployed Inventory (MJDI) and a logistic element on the new joint operational computer system (JC2SS). MJDI will provide the joint stores accounting and management capability in a deployed Theatre.

115. The Department has been frank and open about the difficulties encountered in tracking equipment in theatre. Improvements to this capability are being actively pursued.

We will be interested to see the results of the audit of previously issued body armour components and the action that MOD plans to take in response to the findings. (Paragraph 264).

116. The results of the Enhanced Combat Body Armour (ECBA) audit are detailed in the attached tables, which also include issues data for Combat Body Armour (CBA) Covers (these do not have the pockets for the ECBA plates). The audit has shown that current stockholdings of ECBA components account for 66% of the total number procured since 1992. The remainder (some 38,000 plates, 29,000 fillers and 79,000 'temperate/desert covers) have been consumed over this period of as a result of wear and tear, and operational loss. As can be seen from the data, ECBA is issued as individual components and stocks are held throughout the supply chain at central, single Service and in-theatre storage facilities.

117. When the audit was carried out there were sufficient plates in stock to equip some 48,000 personnel (based on two plates per set of ECBA). The overall number of ECBA/CBA component issues since 1992 (691,458) is broadly consistent with the initial estimate of 700,000 provided in February.

118. The figures for the number of issues include items that have been returned to stock and re-issued, possibly more than once, and therefore indicate the volume of activity rather than the number of items issued on a permanent basis.

119. The data for the audit was collected from a number of sources. Whilst we hold central records of the procurement, issue and central stockholding of ECBA/CBA, information was also collated from the Services, Northern Ireland and Op TELIC to develop a more comprehensive picture of global holdings. Some of this data will have been collected against differing baselines and data on stockholdings can only therefore provide a snapshot in time.

120. Taking into account the lessons learned from operations in Iraq, we are currently in the process of developing a policy for the future issue of ECBA, drawing on that which already exists for other items of personal protection such as the GS helmet and S10 respirator. The results of the ECBA audit will inform this process in terms of the requirement for the initial procurement of ECBA components to support it. Our aim is to have this policy approved by the summer.

TABLE 1: ENHANCED COMBAT BODY ARMOUR

ITEM	SCALING	PROCURED	ISSUED	STOCKHOLDINGS						TOTAL STOCK
				CENTRAL	ARMY	NAVY	RAF	NI	In-Theatre Op TELIC	
Plates	2	134,546	160,866	40,315	8,649	1,771	2,292	18,860	24,536	96,423
Fillers	1	117,402	207,927	23,239	30,488	8,649	6,142	9,861	9,782	88,161
Covers:										
Desert	1	110,499	49,697	46,255	683	432	127	–	22,065	69,562
Temperate	1	69,980	96,510	9,614	5,141	1,087	1,015	10,054	5,037	31,948
Total Covers		180,479	146,207	55,869	5,824	1,519	1,142	10,054	27,102	101,510
Total ECBA Components		432,247	515,000	119,423	44,961	11,939	9,576	38,775	61,420	286,094

Note:

1. There were also 12,146 UN Blue Covers issued, although this item has not been included in the audit.

2. The 515,000 issues detailed above, together with 176,458 issues of CBA temperate and desert covers gives a total issues figure of 691,458 (this excludes relatively small issues of other components detailed at Table 2 Note 4).

TABLE 2: COMBAT BODY ARMOUR (COVERS)

ITEM	SCALING	PROCURED	ISSUED	STOCKHOLDINGS						TOTAL STOCK
				CENTRAL	ARMY	NAVY	RAF	NI	In-Theatre Op TELIC	
Covers:										
Desert	1	–	44,176	80,233	–	139	–	–	2,610	32,982
Temperate	1	–	132,282	71,087	25,275	7,662	1,306	2,986	8	108,324
Total Covers		See Note 2	176,458	101,320	25,275	7,801	1,306	2,986	2,618	141,306

Notes:

1. The CBA figures are included for completeness, however, CBA Covers cannot be used with ECBA.

2. Quantities of CBA Covers procured was not sourced for this audit.

3. Fillers are listed as ECBA (Table 1) as they are common to both.

4. UN Blue (3,105 issued) and Royal Navy Covers (54 held by RN Units) have not been included in this audit. Also omitted were MOD Police Body Armour, Concealed High Velocity Body Armour, Searchers Body Armour and Improved Northern Ireland Body Armour. These are relatively small dependencies and would not materially affect the overall totals.

Before any firm decision on whether enhanced body armour should become a personal issue item is made, the views of service personnel, as well as the logistic implications of a change in policy, must be considered. If the conclusion is that enhanced body armour is not required for all operations, efforts should nonetheless be made to ensure that where it is required it is issued to personnel before their deployment.

121. The Department is currently reviewing its policy on the issue of ECBA. All key stakeholders are being consulted in the exercise. A decision should be made by the summer.

SA80 A2

The modifications to the SA80 have provided UK service personnel with a more effective weapon system. MOD must ensure that users of the weapon are kept fully aware of the cleaning requirements for different environments and provide the necessary cleaning material. Concerns about the weapon's safety catch must be monitored and, where necessary, appropriate action taken. (Paragraph 267).

122. The Department notes the Committee's view of the importance of ensuring that the SA80A2 maintenance regime is promulgated. Reports from Operation TELIC are of almost universal praise for the performance of the SA80A2. The promulgation of the SA80 cleaning regime was reinforced in theatre by providing an additional double aide memoire (cleaning procedure and safety plunger maintenance). We have received no formal reports of stoppages during the operation.

123. The problem with the safety catch/plunger is infrequent, and is very quick to rectify. The problem does not result in catastrophic failure and its onset is gradual.

124. Nevertheless, a new safety plunger has been trialled in Iraq and has been approved following safety certification. 200,000 new safety catches have been ordered. Deliveries will begin in June 2004 and will be completed in March 2005. The intention is to fit the complete SA80A2 fleet with the new plunger.

Ammunition

Our examination suggests that there were problems with the supply of ammunition when the fighting echelon began operations. MOD accepts that in the very early stages there were some problems and not all service personnel had the right amount. We expect MOD to establish the scale of the problem, to investigate any specific cases identified, in particular the tragic incident involving the six Royal Military Policemen, and to implement the necessary action to avoid any re-occurrence in the future. (Paragraph 270).

125. The Department notes the Committee's concerns about the supply of ammunition at the start of operations. Over 23 million rounds of 5.56mm ball ammunition were delivered to Operation TELIC. This was well in excess of the projected requirement of all units deployed. Despite persistent rumours, no shortages of 5.56mm ammunition were reported to HQ 1(UK) Armoured Div by brigades either prior to or after crossing the Line of Departure. While at times during the advance into Iraq the logistic supply chain was

stretched temporarily, the Department has been unable to verify allegations that individual units were left with insufficient ammunition.

126. It is not possible to determine whether some of the rumours relate to troops in rear areas, who may not have been allocated ammunition by their commanders. Notwithstanding this, we have no record of commanders mentioning ammunition shortages in their post-operation reports.

127. There has been speculation about the level of ammunition available to the 6 Royal Military Policemen who died in Al-Majar Al-Kabir on 24 June 2003. In order to establish the facts surrounding this issue, a Board of Inquiry (BOI) convened on 15 March 2004, which is examining the circumstances leading up to the point at which the six soldiers moved into the police station. The BOI will examine weapon and ammunition scalings, and we are confident that this, together with the Service Police investigation, will provide a much clearer understanding of events.

Night Vision Capability

"We understand that MOD is currently reviewing the scales of issue of night vision equipment. We consider that the ability to operate confidently and effectively at night greatly enhances force protection and capability. We look to MOD to examine the case for providing night vision capability to all service personnel who are required to operate at night. (Paragraph 272)."

128. The Department has a number of programmes that are designed to improve our forces' night vision capability. The Head Mounted Night Visions System programme provides individual night vision equipment for infantry units as well as the RAF Regiment and 3 Commando Brigade. The procurement of this system was accelerated through UOR action and has proved to be particularly effective on operations in Afghanistan and Iraq. The Light Weight Thermal Imaging programme provides a thermal imaging capability at platoon level in infantry units as well as the RAF Regiment and 3 Commando Brigade. We also plan to procure a Surveillance System and Range Finder that will provide an integrated TI and laser range finder which will equip fire controllers within the combat and combat support arms of the Army as well as the RAF Regiment and 3 Commando Brigade. These three programmes, in combination, will provide a significant enhancement to the ability of our forces to operate at night.

NBC Equipment

We find it alarming that MOD had to 'move Combopens around in theatre' to fulfil the requirement. (Paragraph 274).

129. Redistribution of 'Combopens' around theatre to ensure that the individuals requiring such personal protection received it was a sensible response to the protection needs of UK forces.

Given the potential threat posed by Iraqi armed forces, sufficient chemical warfare detection and protection were particularly important for this operation. However, there were serious shortcomings in the supply and distribution system and the required

levels of detection and protection were not always available to everyone. Indeed, while MOD ideally would have liked each serviceman and woman to have had four suits available, only one suit per person was available which MOD judged to be sufficient for this operation. Furthermore it is essential that personnel have confidence in the effectiveness of the equipment with which they are provided. It was fortuitous that service personnel did not suffer as a consequence, but had the Iraqis used chemical weapons systematically, as employed in the Iran-Iraq war, the operational consequences would have been severe. The lack of armoured vehicle filters seems to us to be a matter of the utmost seriousness. The lessons identified need to be implemented as a matter of urgency to ensure that servicemen and women serving on operations have complete and justified confidence that chemical warfare attacks will be detected in time, that their individual protection equipment will save their lives and that operational success will not be imperilled. This is particularly important given that UK service personnel are more likely to be operating in such environments in the future. (Paragraph 281).

130. The NAO report on Operation TELIC states: "Although overall protection against chemical agents was good there were shortfalls". This is the position that the Department has set out consistently since the operation began. There were sufficient stocks on the shelf for all personnel who deployed into theatre, including contractors and embedded journalists. Notwithstanding this, owing to a mismatch between the sizes of the suits and individuals, a small number of troops crossed the Line of Departure with only one properly fitting suit. In particular there was a shortage of large suits which primarily affected the Irish Guards. This was caused by a combination of out-of-date sizing information and a lack of historical data. We have developed procedures with PJHQ to ensure units do not take in excess of their requirement in the future, and are increasing the on-the-shelf size range.

131. Commanders assessed that the risk posed to the Force by these shortages was low. The effect on morale was judged to be more serious than the practical impact.

132. For NBC filter on armoured vehicles, as with other threats, we had to judge the balance of risk between waiting for all equipment to arrive and be available and delaying the start of combat operations. Although a limited number of NBC vehicle filters for some types of vehicle had arrived in 1 (UK) Division before hostilities began, these had to compete with other priorities such as in-theatre integration of forces and receiving and integrating the final two armoured Battlegroups into the Division.

133. Not all armoured vehicles have NBC filters fitted. For example older designs such as most of the FV430 series and some of Combat Vehicle Reconnaissance (Tracked) variants do not. Our principal fighting vehicles, such as Challenger 2, Warrior and AS90 do. Sufficient NBC filters were dispatched to Iraq, most in time for operations, but problems with asset tracking in theatre meant that these were unable to be located until after hostilities had ceased.

134. However, troops are trained to operate armoured vehicles wearing their personal NBC equipment, irrespective of whether the vehicle has collective NBC protection.

Logistics and Asset Tracking

Given how critical logistics are to operations, we expect MOD to implement the lessons identified in its reports on Operation TELIC, and also those lessons identified by the National Audit Office. We intend to closely monitor the progress of MOD's end-to-end review. (Paragraph 283).

135. There is a clear process for capturing Lessons Identified from Operations and exercises led by the Defence Operational Capability audit team. National Audit Office (NAO) and other reports will also be collated to ensure a comprehensive compendium of lessons' material for consideration in our forward plans. One of the End-to-End Review's recommendations reinforced CDL's appointment as end-to-end (E2E) Logistic Process Owner for the Department. In addition, the Defence Logistics Board has been established. The Board provides strategic direction to develop an operationally effective E2E support chain that delivers operational and logistic effect, aiming to give the end user full confidence. It provides clear guidance on immediate priorities, and offers direction to develop future logistic capabilities. The aim is to give primacy to operational effectiveness at all times, without sacrificing the overall need for efficiency.

We are in no doubt that one of the key lessons to emerge from Operation TELIC concerns operational logistic support and specifically, the requirement for a robust system to track equipment and stocks both into and within theatre—a requirement which was identified in the 1991 Gulf War. The lack of such a system on Operation TELIC resulted in numerous problems with the in-theatre distribution of critical items such as ammunition, body armour and NBC equipment. MOD has told us that having such a system is top of its logistics priorities and we understand that proposals will be submitted to Ministers in the spring. We urge Ministers to provide the necessary funding. However, we find it alarming that a full system is unlikely to be in place within the next five years. (Paragraph 291).

136. Both the NAO report and the Department's own reports on Operation TELIC recognise shortcomings in our ability to track equipment in theatre, and the issue of tracking has been examined. A package of improvements for logistics materiel management has been identified which includes tracking. This package would require funding and options will need to be considered as part of the Department's planning round against other priorities. If funded, the enhancements will provide a robust tracking capability.

Personnel Issues

Accommodation and Food

We are pleased to learn that the majority of Armed Forces personnel in Iraq are now in satisfactory air-conditioned accommodation. Such accommodation is vital in ensuring that Armed Forces personnel can perform their roles effectively when they are deployed to harsh environments. It should be a priority of any operation that appropriate accommodation is made available as quickly as possible. (Paragraph 296).

137. The importance of air conditioning in an exceptionally hot climate is fully appreciated and led to the current level of provisioning across Iraq. In general terms, whilst a comprehensive air conditioned environment might seem desirable, provisioning will always depend on the operational context and priorities. It is also important not to undermine the acclimatisation process, as our Service personnel must retain their ability to operate in harsh environments. The key priority is to provide air conditioned respites, which should be made available as early as possible after the deployment of initial forces. Thereafter, other areas for air conditioning (including some domestic accommodation, offices and communal areas) will follow on in due course.

During our visit to Iraq we were impressed with the quality of the food provided to our Armed Forces, particularly given the difficult conditions, such as the very high temperatures, in which catering personnel had to work. (Paragraph 299).

138. The production of high quality food is a team effort involving not only the DLO and the World Wide Food contractor '3663' but also the unit chefs who consistently produce a high standard in the most difficult of conditions.

Operational Welfare Package and Families

We regret the decision to withdraw the free postal service in February 2004. (Paragraph 300).

139. The decision to withdraw the free postal packet scheme became effective on 8 April 2004, but affects neither the free delivery of aerogramme letters nor of electronic letters.

140. The free postal packet scheme allowed friends and relatives of named Service personnel to send a packet[1] weighing less than 2kg in weight to the Iraq theatre of operations free of charge. A number of factors influenced the introduction of the temporary scheme:

- During the First Gulf War the British public demonstrated their support for Service personnel by donating gifts of toiletries, books and small consumables. The scale of the support overwhelmed both the British Forces Post Office and the logistic supply chain. Many boxes were eventually buried by the side of the road and a large number were diverted to stations within the United Kingdom. It was identified that the absence of a specific addressee was a contributory factor in this.

- When the scheme was introduced on 17 April 2003 Service personnel, fighting in particularly austere conditions, did not have access to the welfare facilities and consumables that are now available and the desire of the British public to demonstrate support for Service personnel in Iraq was at its highest[2].

141. Initially, the Royal Mail Group paid for the cost of transport between the point of posting and delivery to the British Forces Post Office. The subsidy ceased in July 2003.

---

[1] In Royal Mail Group terminology a packet is 2kg or less, a parcel weighs more than 2kg.

[2] After the introduction of the free service, volumes of mail despatched to theatre had to be limited to 20 tons per day, double the amount usually handled. By October 2003, 3 tons of mail was being dispatched to theatre of which 2 tons were packets; this figure remains constant.

Following careful consideration, including consultation with the chain of command, the scheme was discontinued in April, coinciding with the roulement of 20 Armd Bde and 1 Mech Bde.

142. The free postal packet service was a measure unique to Iraq; no other overseas or UK based operation receives a similar concession. Given that the provision of goods and services in Iraq has reached the expected standard, and is similar to those found on other operations, it would be wholly divisive to continue to offer the service only to those in Iraq especially as the welfare facilities available in theatre have been described as 'the envy of US forces'. Those items that the scheme most commonly catered for are now commonly available in theatre and the complete welfare package includes:

- Free aerogramme letters and e-letters ('blueys' and 'e-blueys').

- A free 20 minute phone call to anywhere in the world once a week (this can be supplemented by the purchase of additional phone cards).

- Free Internet access.

- Packets up to 2kg in weight may be sent at a reduced cost equivalent to the UK Inland First Class Postage Rate[3].

- A generous allocation of TVs and radios to watch/listen to multi-channel British Forces Broadcasting Services TV /radio along with Videos, DVDs and computer games.

- Free books/newspapers and magazines.

- Free board games.

- Access to the Expeditionary Forces Institute that will deliver a service across the British area of responsibility.

- Access to basic leisure facilities off duty (gymnasium/fitness equipment, coffee bars and 'Wetherspoon' style pubs).

- Access to a Combined Services Entertainment show once during a 6-month tour.

- A visit by a showbiz personality once during a 6-month tour.

- Two weeks Rest and Recuperation during a 6-month tour with an additional four weeks leave at the end of a six-month tour.

- Extra allowances for deployment away from the home base.

- Issue of additional travel warrants to spouses to enable them to visit family members.

---

[3] A first class stamp will be required for cards; the cost will rise according to weight to a maximum of 2kg for which £6.89 will be charged. This was previously notified as £7.23.

- Allocation of £1 per week for every person deployed on operations to Units to enable welfare facilities (such as Internet cafes) to be established for partners and families to use at the home base.

143. All of this comes at a cost to the taxpayer and schemes such as free postal packets must be seen in the context of the complete package now available to Service personnel. When the scheme finishes between £1.5m - £2m will have been spent providing free postal packets. Should the scheme continue, it would be invidious not to extend it to all operational personnel (and the Iraq theatre of operations represents a third of those currently deployed on operations). Under these circumstances we could not guarantee postal delivery on RAF flights to the theatre in question and would have to resort to civil charter with increased costs. Dependant on the numbers involved in operations and the availability of RAF transport this could cost between £3m -£9m pa. In order to fund this, savings would have to be made in other, more essential, elements of the Operational Welfare Package, which would be highly undesirable.

The Operational Welfare Package (OWP) in place for Operation TELIC worked well and was well received. However, we are concerned that early entry forces saw little benefit from the package. MOD acknowledges that this is an area where improvements are needed. We expect MOD to implement such improvements as quickly as possible. (Paragraph 302).

144. The second edition of the Operational Welfare Support Policies' Compendium, dated 19 March 2004, includes a requirement for an OWP for early entry forces and PJHQ will be responsible for delivering this. Concurrently, PJHQ produced a Concept of Operations brief for early entry welfare communications. Moreover, a trial was conducted in Norway in March 2004 with the supporting contractor and elements of 3 Cdo Bde provided with a satellite phone linked laptop e-mail messaging service. Following this trial, 40 ruggedised laptops have been acquired to meet the requirement of one of the assigned Spearhead Battalion Groups. Final validation work will be undertaken in late April/May 2004 by forces deployed in Afghanistan. Together with an operational reserve of Iridium satellite phones a solution to the requirement for both voice and basic e-mail welfare communications has now been identified and, subject to validation activity, this combination will be an invaluable welfare enhancement. Work on the provision of the leisure/relaxation element of the OWP for early entry forces is also in train.

We are pleased to learn that the needs of families are being addressed and that there is now a families element to the operational welfare package. (Paragraph 305).

145. The Operational Welfare Package is based on a Review of Operational Welfare which reported in late 1999. The subsequent publicly-funded policy was issued in the summer 2002 and most recently reviewed and updated in March 2004. The policy is clear in its four key component requirements and deliverables which are: Communications; Leisure/relaxation; Physiological and Families. Of these, the communications package (20 mins telephone call-time per week per person; Internet access, personal e-mail; a postal service by letter, free aerogrammes (blueys) and e-blueys (further enhanced in 2003 by the forces post card)) is designed to link those deployed with home and is identified as key in maintaining and improving the morale of our Service personnel and their operational effectiveness. Further links with families are supported by:

- Concessionary postal rates;

- Concessionary travel for families;

- The operational welfare leaflet (to ensure Service personnel and their families are fully briefed on the OWP and allowances that they will be eligible for once deployed);

- The introduction in April 2003 of the Family Package.

146. The Family Package assists Home Units in providing welfare support to families of Service Personnel deployed on operations. It is applicable to a Home/Parent Unit with at least five personnel deployed on operations, exercises or deployments (for which the OWP has been authorised) and consists of £1 per week for each deployed Service person who is in receipt of OWP. The command will judge the best use of the monies to support activities that enhance communication or relieve hardship that have been generated by the deployment. Expenditure must be within the spirit of this enhancement and be consistent with current guidance on financial propriety and regularity. Examples of acceptable expenditure are:

- Provision of communications equipment (Internet facilities and telephone lines) for Help Information Volunteer Exchanges (HIVE) and Community Centres.

- Meeting the cost of extended Community/Welfare communications (Internet line usage to deployed operation area).

- Assistance towards the costs of producing and posting welfare information (leaflets, flyers and updates).

- Extension of Help Information and Volunteer Exchange (HIVE) opening hours.

- Occasional provision of transport for attendance at briefings/meetings.

- Meeting costs of occasional children's activities (e.g. provision of a crèche during family briefings/meetings).

- Provision of non-alcoholic refreshments at unit-organised briefings/meetings related to the operation.

MOD is currently considering further ways of providing improved information to families. Given how important this is to families, MOD should implement the improvements identified as quickly as possible. (Paragraph 306).

147. The MOD notes and supports the recommendation and recognises the importance of communications between families, those deployed on operations and the Services. The Operational Welfare Package has gone a long way to address communications and continues to improve its delivery. The provision of funds via the OWP family package has enabled flyers, newsletters and briefings (amongst other events) to be delivered at unit level. Other non-operational welfare initiatives such as the continuing development of Services' websites are actively being pursued and put in place. Further, wider, work is also in hand on this issue.

The families of reservists have not, in the past, received the same level of support as the families of regular service personnel. We recommend that MOD takes action to address this imbalance. This is particularly important given the increased contribution which reservists are now making and are expected to make to future operations. (Paragraph 309).

148. A Families Welfare Support Enhancement was introduced on 1 April 2003. This amounts to £1/week/deployed reservist. In the event of a service related death, payments equivalent to attributable benefits will be payable to unmarried partners (where there is a substantial relationship) of reserve personnel. Moreover, the single Services have taken the following action:

- The RN are currently considering the introduction of mobilised Welfare Officers to assist with looking after the families of mobilised reservists.

- HQ LAND has instructed TA units that they may mobilise a TA Unit Welfare Officer. Evidence shows that the Welfare Officer is used to keep in touch with families, visit families and assisting the PSAOs in dealing with any queries from families. A course is run at Bristol University for the Welfare Officers.

- The RAF sends an Information pack to families of reservists prior to their return. The RAFCom Internet website provides a wide range of information for families. Nominated points of contact (RAuxAF have stay behind cells who acted as poc for families. Ex Reg Reserve have a nominated poc from affiliated unit who will be in touch with families) have also been introduced. Finally, regular briefings are given to families.

MOD needs to ensure that service personnel have access to the required level of life and accident insurance while on operations. (Paragraph 310).

149. After the events of 9/11 insurers reviewed their exposure to risk in the light of global terrorism, WMD proliferation and operational tempo. Accordingly, much of the limited capital has migrated to civilian risks and Life Insurance capacity for our Armed Forces reduced, since Service risks are deemed *'unquantifiable'*.

150. Several major providers (e.g. the PAX (personal accident) scheme with some 62,000 members) have introduced exclusions for nuclear risks, biological and chemical weapons or 'dirty' bombs; others have withdrawn schemes. These exclusions affect death benefits under accident policies.

151. During Operation TELIC some Service personnel—especially reservists—faced exclusions for some of the specific war risks they faced and some failed to secure appropriate cover before deploying.

152. MOD provides a comprehensive compensation package through the Armed Forces Pension Scheme (AFPS) and the War Pensions Scheme. Even the refocused AFPS arrangements—which will not be widely applicable for many years—may not always match desired levels of financial security, particularly for junior people with large responsibilities.

153. People requiring enhanced benefit levels were previously able to buy optional Life Insurance. Although Life Insurance schemes are now available to Service personnel, comprehensive cover is not universal—particularly for the large accumulated numbers of Regulars and Reservists.

154. We recognise that gaps in commercial life insurance cover are an important area where action is needed, but a decision on whether a commitment to support a Group Life Insurance scheme for our Armed Forces would be justified has yet to be taken. However, options for an appropriate Departmental solution are currently under consideration.

Bereavement

We conclude that, overall, MOD's casualty reporting arrangements worked well during Operation TELIC. We emphasise the critical importance of ensuring that next of kin are informed of any casualty by the MOD and not the media. We welcome the improvements in the revised arrangements introduced, which now better reflect the needs of bereaved families. (Paragraph 316).

155. We welcome the comments of the HCDC and have nothing to add.

We welcome the fact that widows' benefits have been extended to unmarried partners of service personnel who die in conflict, and that bereaved families can now remain in their service accommodation until they are ready to leave. We look to MOD to implement any further improvements which are identified by the current tri-Service review of bereavement policy. (Paragraph 318).

156. The Department is conducting a 'Training-Needs-Analysis' of the training given to Service personnel nominated to assist bereaved families in the aftermath of a death in-Service. This will assess current provision, identify areas that could be improved upon and will enable us to promote 'best practice' across the Department. Furthermore, a Guide for Bereaved families is about to be published, which has been designed to assist widows and bereaved families and explain the welfare provision available from the Services. Drafts of this Guide were circulated to Service Widows Associations for comment and this initiative has been welcomed.

Training

The high number of operations which UK service personnel have been involved in has had an adverse impact on their training. We expect MOD to ensure that service personnel returning from operations catch up with their training as soon as possible and that promotion opportunities are not adversely affected because of their operational deployment. But we recognise that, in the short term, the most important point is for service personnel to recuperate properly and that this includes the opportunity to take the leave to which they are entitled. However, the Government must recognise that the Armed Forces are simply not large enough to sustain the pattern of operational deployment since the Strategic Defence Review permanently without serious risk of damage to their widely admired professional standards. (Paragraph 320).

157. Assumptions about the concurrency of operations are based on historical analysis of the type, scale and endurance of recent deployments, together with a judgement about how this pattern might evolve in future. As a norm and without creating overstretch we should be able to mount an enduring medium scale peace support operation simultaneously with a small scale peace support operation and a one-off small scale intervention operation.

158. We may choose to do more than this, accepting that there will be an impact on training and individual or collective 'harmony' (single Service guidelines on the length and frequency of operational deployments):

- We should be able to reconfigure our forces rapidly to carry out the enduring medium and small scale peace support operations simultaneously with a limited duration medium scale intervention operation.

- Given time to prepare we should be able to reconfigure to conduct a large-scale operation while still conducting a small scale enduring operation and fulfilling standing commitments.

159. Operation TELIC preceded by Operation FRESCO placed unusually high demands on our Armed Forces.

160. We recognise that the high level of personnel committed to operations has made attendance on promotional courses difficult, but there is the capacity to cope with the 'peaks and troughs' of the educational demand of personnel deploying on, or recuperating from operations, therefore not disadvantaging officers and soldiers in terms of promotion opportunities.

161. The importance of individuals being able to take the leave to which they are entitled to should not be underestimated. This was problematic for Operation TELIC, as some units, especially those who had been committed to Operation FRESCO, were unable to take their Post Operational Tour Leave (POTL) and annual leave Entitlement. We recognise that it is imperative for our troops to recuperate and these situations have been closely monitored, exploiting every opportunity for individuals to take their leave entitlement.

Post Operation Health

We are pleased to hear that MOD has commissioned research into the physical and psychological health of personnel who deployed and that the initial research is being followed up in a major study to commence early this year. We look forward to seeing the outcome of this work and expect MOD to take appropriate action in response to its findings. (Paragraph 322).

162. The major study, based on an initial questionnaire which is being sent out to about 19,000 personnel, is underway. Results are expected by the end of 2004 and will be published in the peer-reviewed scientific literature.

163. Further stages of the research will depend on the results of the questionnaire, but might include clinical studies and a comparison of the findings with the results of the Exposures Study being undertaken by the Institute for Environment and Health. This

study aims to collect and examine data and records from Operation TELIC, including operation logs, to identify possible exposures that may have adverse health effects.

164. In order to ensure the independence of the research, an oversight board, including scientists recommended by the Medical Research Council and the Economic and Social Research Council and representatives from the Royal British Legion, has been set up. The Board overseas the research, and will also advise the MOD on any future research it thinks necessary.

We are pleased to learn that the take up and use of the new medical form appears to have been high and that, despite the increased administrative burden, it has proved popular with users. We note that MOD is reviewing the format in order to ensure even greater utility for future operations. (Paragraph 323).

165. We are pleased that the introduction of the new medical form has proved to be a success. Our review will make the form even more user-friendly for future operations

We welcome the measures relating to post traumatic stress disorder which MOD introduced for Operation TELIC. We look to MOD to monitor this aspect closely and also other illnesses experienced as a result of being deployed on Operation TELIC. We are disappointed by the delays to the publication of MOD's paper covering the health lessons from Operation GRANBY and the experience of Operation TELIC. Given the level of interest in these matters, we expect MOD to publish this paper as soon as possible. (Paragraph 327).

166. We are confident that the measures we are now putting in to place to create a managed health system, including the creation of Departments of Community Mental Health and the use of private providers for in-patient mental health care, will enhance our ability to monitor post-traumatic stress disorder and other illnesses experienced as a result of being deployed on Operation TELIC.

167. The paper on the health lessons identified since the 1991 Gulf Conflict was initially only intended to include lessons from Operation GRANBY; however it was decided to delay the publication of the paper so that it can take into account the experience of Operation TELIC. The paper will be published soon.

Costs and Recovery

Resource Accounting and Budgeting

Resource Accounting and Budgeting (RAB) is a complex financial process and MOD needs to ensure that its staff are appropriately trained in its application. We remain concerned that the application of RAB may, perhaps through a misinterpretation of its aim, have led to stock holdings being reduced too far. We recommend that MOD undertakes a review which assesses whether RAB is leading to poor decision making, in particular in relation to stock level holdings. (Paragraph 333).

168. The Department constantly reviews its stock and Capital Spares holdings against assessments of future requirements to minimise unnecessary overheads. These are business

based judgements and we do not believe that RAB has in itself had a significant impact on decisions about levels of stock holding.

169. Deciding on appropriate levels of stock holdings is a complex process which requires careful balancing of risks and costs. In particular, ensuring value for money within a finite resource budget requires us to balance the need to hold stocks in store against the practicality of obtaining stocks from industry, or elsewhere, within anticipated warning and preparation times. The MOD carries out regular detailed Logistic Sustainability and Deployability Audits to review, and where necessary update, its stockpile requirements and holdings. For key consumable stocks (such as Enhanced Combat Body Armour, clothing and operational ration packs) the logistic sustainability requirements have been updated, procurement authorised and the modest, non-cash holding costs funded.

Cost of the Operation

It will be some time before the costs of the operation in 2003–04 are known—perhaps not until late summer 2004 when they are published in MOD's Annual Report and Accounts. MOD acknowledges that it has taken longer than expected to assess the costs of stock consumed and equipment lost or damaged during the conflict phase. We expect MOD to ensure this work is advanced as quickly as possible and for the outcome to be reported to Parliament as soon as it is completed. (Paragraph 339).

170. Work on finalising the costs of Operation TELIC in Financial Year 03/04 is being taken forward as quickly as possible with data being audited by the National Audit Office as part of their audit of the MOD's 2003/04 Accounts. Final figures will be included in the Department's Annual Report and Accounts to be published in September, in line with the accounts of other Government Departments.

We expect MOD to recover costs owed to them by other Coalition partners as soon as possible. (Paragraph 340).

171. Cost recovery arrangements are in place and working successfully for current multi-national operations in Iraq. Cost recovery for earlier phases of Operation TELIC is largely complete. Fuel supplied by the UK to US forces, and vice versa, is covered by a number of reciprocal Fuel Exchange Agreements which provide access to each other's fuel stocks. The various FEAs are periodically reconciled and, once all transactions have been agreed, any outstanding balances are cleared by either repayment in kind, or financial reimbursement.

Funding of the Operation

We expect MOD to replace the equipment, and the stores and supplies, necessary to restore the operational capabilities consumed or lost during Operation TELIC as soon as possible, to ensure that Armed Forces personnel can undertake their roles effectively. (Paragraph 344).

172. The Department has now entered a period of recuperation, which is designed to restore required levels of operational capability as soon as practicable. This process includes, as one element of a number of strands of work, action to replace key equipment that has been destroyed and to replenish ammunition and other stores used during

Operation TELIC. As the Department has indicated to the Committee in oral evidence, not all of the individual equipments lost during operations need to be replaced on a like for like basis to meet our recuperation plans. Nor is it sensible for all such replacement or stock replenishment to be taken forward at a uniform rate; rather the pace of recuperation in individual capability areas will reflect a range of factors including the relative contribution to overall levels of operational readiness and the speed with which new stock or equipment can be delivered.

Transition and Reconstruction

Plans and Preparations

Being a junior partner in a Coalition constrained the British Government in its ability to plan independently for after the conflict. (Paragraph 355).

173. The UK worked closely with the US from Autumn 2002 to ensure that contingency planning included planning for the post-conflict phase. Since we were working with the US, it was important that UK and US planning was conducted jointly, as far as possible, rather than for the US and UK to plan independently.

Constraints

We believe that it was a misjudgement by the Government to have decided that planning to meet the needs of the Iraqi people following a conflict was particularly sensitive—more sensitive, even, than the deploying of military forces. This misjudgement unnecessarily constrained planning for the post-conflict phase. (Paragraph 357).

174. The Prime Minister made clear in his statement of 24 September 2002 the need for preparedness and prudent planning. The details of such planning, including for the post-conflict phase, were necessarily sensitive as some information about the military plan could be extrapolated from details of the post-conflict plan. Furthermore, as our witnesses have explained, we felt that overt planning for the post-conflict would make it appear that military action was inevitable (which it was not) and could seriously prejudice ongoing attempts to reach a diplomatic solution. This should not be taken to imply, however, that robust planning was constrained. Rather that it was necessarily confined to a limited number of people.

175. DFID also led on preparations for a range of humanitarian contingencies, though fortunately no humanitarian crisis transpired. No secret was made of this work and plans were set out on a number of occasions, not least in the written statement to Parliament by the Secretary of State for International Development on 13 March 2003.

176. What was more sensitive were some of the details of post-conflict planning with international organisations and non-governmental organisations (NGOs), many of whom DFID had funded in order to be prepared for the possibility of conflict. Several of these organisations were understandably reluctant to admit openly that they were engaging in post-conflict planning and we respected these concerns. This meant that some of the details of their plans were not publicised, but this did not significantly constrain our

planning process. In the event, for both security and political reasons, international organisations and NGOs were not able to play as strong a post-conflict role in Iraq as we had hoped. As the government has acknowledged, we also under-estimated the degree of breakdown in law and order which followed the fall of Saddam's regime.

It has also been suggested that DfID's role in post-conflict planning was constrained by the attitude of the then Secretary of State towards the prospect of military action. Although our witness from DfID denied that this was the case, we remain to be convinced. (Paragraph 358).

177. The government undertook considerable post-conflict planning in the run-up to military action. DFID participated closely in this cross-government process, including through its secondment of advisers to the British military and the Office of Reconstruction and Humanitarian Assistance in Kuwait, and to the cross-departmental Iraq Planning Unit based in the FCO.

The poor co-ordination of planning within the US Administration meant that better co-ordinated British input into the process had less impact than it should have had. (Paragraph 362).

178. Whilst the arrangements for co-ordination of post conflict planning—which by its very nature is a complicated and multi-faceted business involving an enormous range of issues and requiring input from a large number of people with different areas of expertise—within the much larger US system may initially have been uncertain, we do not believe that this significantly diminished the influence which our own thinking had on the overall planning. Planning work done by the UK may have been one factor which helped the US to reach a view on how to best to approach the issues. When co-ordination mechanisms were agreed the UK was able to make an important contribution to the Coalition plan.

The need to maintain a unified Iraq under central control has been a constraint— usually a reasonable constraint—on British freedom of action in the south-east of the country. (Paragraph 364).

179. UK leadership of Multinational Division South-East and the CPA regional coordinating office in Basrah clearly has to be within the context of policies made in Baghdad. However, Multinational Divisions and CPA regional offices do have latitude in the way that they implement those policies.

Perversely, the failure of the wider international community to support the Coalition's military action did little or nothing to constrain that action, but did make it more difficult for the Coalition to restore law and order and to administer Iraq once hostilities were over. (Paragraph 365).

180. We agree that the absence of some international organisations usually active in post-conflict situations did have some effect on immediate post-conflict efforts.

Planning Assumptions for the Transitional Phase

The Government was right to plan for a humanitarian crisis. Such a situation might have arisen, and the Government would have been rightly condemned if its preparations had been inadequate. (Paragraph 369).

181. We agree.

For the Government to argue that it was unaware of the extent of the repressive brutality of the Iraqi regime strains credibility. It was widely known, not least because of information published by the Government. (Paragraph 375).

182. The Government was not arguing that it was unaware of the extent of the repressive brutality of the Iraqi regime but rather that it was difficult to predict in detail what would happen after the regime's removal. In particular the impact on relatively low-level Iraqi administrative structures was greater than we had expected.

Insecurity and Disorder in the Transitional Phase

Much has been made of the many Iraqis who were involved in looting and destruction in the immediate aftermath of the removal of Saddam Hussein's regime. It should not be forgotten that thousands more were locked up indoors fearing for their security and for their lives. (Paragraph 379).

183. We agree. The establishment of basic law and order was initially hindered both by the other demands on Coalition manpower, including continuing combat operations, and by the unexpectedly large-scale disintegration of local Iraqi authorities including the police.

The scale and shape of the force provided were best suited to achieving the Coalition's desired effects in the combat phase, but not to carrying those effects through into the post-conflict phase. We acknowledge, however, that the scale of force which might have best achieved these effects was beyond the Government's means. (Paragraph 387).

184. It is obviously true that there are limits to the scale of force we could possibly have deployed. We have also acknowledged that the extent to which Iraqi police and armed forces effectively dissolved themselves was greater than we had expected.

A harsh critic might argue that Coalition planning assumed that it would be possible to employ elements of the Iraqi police, army and administration to maintain law and order, because the alternatives were too difficult to contemplate. That assumption was not only incorrect, but incautious. A realistic judgement, based on good intelligence, should have warned of the risk of serious disorder. (Paragraph 388).

185. The issue of maintaining law and order was recognised and much work was undertaken on predicting the alternative outcomes if disorder occurred. But it should be remembered that the Coalition's intention had always been to enable a rapid transition to Iraqi rule, and the assumption that some elements of Iraqi forces could be quickly co-opted should be seen in this light.

It was indeed crucial to protect Iraq's oil infrastructure from damage, as the main potential source of future Iraqi wealth. But it was a mistake not to have identified and protected (and to have been seen to be protecting) other key buildings and infrastructure as a priority. (Paragraph 390).

186. It would have been literally impossible to have protected every single building of the sort which attracted the attention of looters, without much greater levels of manpower. As we have noted, the virtual disappearance of the Iraqi police and armed forces, combined with other demands on Coalition forces while combat operations were continuing in some areas, contributed to the difficulties the Coalition experienced initially in establishing law and order. Protecting the oil and power system was a priority for both environmental and economic reasons.

If 'a few more' troops were needed to protect key sites, this should have been identified as a scenario at the planning stage, and these troops should have been found and deployed with this specific task in mind. (Paragraph 392).

187. As we note above, it would not have been possible to protect all key sites and prioritisation was necessary. This is not unusual and the solution was to sequence resources and adopt local police to enhance security, engaging the Iraqis in providing for their own security needs. As the Committee has identified, there were joint Iraqi/Coalition patrols within the first week of the campaign. The early difficulties reflected the initial problems encountered in getting Iraqi police officers re-engaged in the task of providing law and order.

The Government should have taken more care to identify in advance sites in Iraq likely to contain records of use to the Coalition, and should have ensured that forces were provided to protect these sites from damage and looting. (Paragraph 397).

188. The issue of trying to obtain records of use to the Coalition was recognised as important. However, Iraq was a difficult intelligence target and detailed information about the locations of such records was not available.

While Coalition forces successfully removed Saddam Hussein's regime with remarkable speed, they were not able to establish themselves on the ground with sufficient speed and precision to avoid a damaging period of lawlessness during which much of the potential goodwill of the Iraqi people was squandered. (Paragraph 398).

189. We agree that the early law and order problems were damaging, although we believe that the position was stabilised fairly quickly in most parts of the country.

None of these criticisms, however, should be seen to detract from the thoroughly impressive way in which individual members of Armed Forces personnel demonstrated their ability to accomplish the transition between warfighting and peacekeeping operations swiftly and effectively. (Paragraph 399).

190. We agree that the UK Armed Forces personnel adapted quickly and effectively to peacekeeping operations at the end of the end of major combat operations. Their performance since that time has again demonstrated their professionalism and versatility.

We commend the International Committee of the Red Cross (ICRC) for the performance of its humanitarian role in Iraq, before, during and after the combat phase of operations, and we commend British forces for the way in which they cooperated with the ICRC. (Paragraph 402).

191. We are grateful for the Committee's observations.

Lessons for Future Campaigns

We recommend that the Government should consider closely, in the light of operations in Iraq, how the United Kingdom provides peace support capabilities, and in particular how the transition is managed between warfighting and peacekeeping. We further recommend that the Government should consider whether either a dedicated part of the Armed Forces, or even a separate organisation altogether, could be specifically tasked with providing these capabilities. (Paragraph 407).

192. The UK MOD generates peace support capability as part of military capability. UK Forces are trained and equipped to carry out peacekeeping, Peace Support Operations and warfighting operations as an integral part of a campaign, and often have to transition between these scenarios, as in Iraq. As the Chief of the General Staff stated to the Committee, recent operational experience has shown that a deployed force may be involved in warfighting, peacekeeping and humanitarian operations simultaneously, the so-called '3-block war'. The best way to prepare for the demands of this type of operation is to train primarily for warfighting. In modern operations there is no clear transition between warfighting and peacekeeping and it would therefore incur unnecessary operational risk to employ a dedicated part of the Armed Forces solely for peace support operations.

193. Transition from conflict to post-conflict situations is a wider issue for the Government, and national and international objectives for such complex operations cannot be achieved solely by military forces. Indeed, other Government Departments, multinational organisations and the private sector are essential elements, particularly for the process of rebuilding security, social and economic infrastructures. Lessons identified from Operation TELIC, as from other recent operations, have highlighted the need for a multi-agency approach.

194. There are many activities underway across Whitehall to consider methods of better coordinating national efforts in conflict scenarios, for both the conflict prevention stages (including through the Conflict Prevention Pool), and for military-civilian transitions and post conflict reconstruction. Meanwhile a cross-departmental working group (FCO, MOD and DFID) has been set up to consider ways in which to improve UK planning, co-ordination and management of post conflict reconstruction activities.

We are concerned about the continuing requirement on the ground for specialists from the military in areas which would under other circumstances be provided by civilian organisations. Many of these specialists will be reservists, and their prolonged deployment may have adverse consequences for retention in specialisms which are already suffering from undermanning. (Paragraph 411).

195. In the main, reservists have not been called-out specifically to fill specialist civilian administration roles. Only two reservists who volunteered to be mobilised have been called-out specifically for their civilian skills. For the rest, the fact that they possessed skills associated with their civilian employment which could be utilised during the reconstruction of Iraq was fortunate, but not planned. This is a prime example of the benefits that reservists bring to the Armed Forces. With regard to "prolonged deployments" in general reservists have served no longer than six months in Iraq. A small number have served longer, but this is because they volunteered to do so. We do not believe that this will have an adverse effect on retention.

196. The work referred to in the response to recommendation 111 should reduce the need to use reservists for these purposes. We are also conscious that post-conflict operations in Iraq are unusual in that the UK is Occupying Power with the full range of responsibilities which that involves.

We agree that the provision of language training will need to be re-examined if the Armed Forces are to be more involved in expeditionary operations in the future. In an effects-based operation aiming to win over hearts and minds, an ability to communicate with the local population is vital. (Paragraph 414).

197. We agree. Language training is currently being reviewed through a series of processes which will produce an effective and efficient way of achieving this objective.

Preparations should have been made in advance of the military campaign to ensure that police advice on maintaining law and order would be available as soon as possible after the end of the combat phase. (Paragraph 416).

198. The Government accepts that we underestimated the extent of civil disorder problems that we would face and the dislocation of Iraqi civil administrative structures. However, we quickly adapted to the situation, and deployed civilian police advisers from the beginning of July. The security situation prevented us from deploying a large civilian police force before then. We have been undertaking substantial work to build Iraqi security capability ever since. There are now almost 80,000 Iraqi police. This is a very important step towards gradually giving responsibility for security in Iraq to Iraqis as their capability increases.

While we support entirely the notion that Iraqis should be encouraged to take responsibility for their own security, we are concerned that local militias which have been allowed to operate in the south-east of Iraq may represent vested interests. There is a danger that these may seek to use their position to pursue agendas which might not be to the advantage of the people of Iraq more generally. (Paragraph 417).

199. We agree with the Committee that in the long-term, allowing independent militias to operate unchecked in Iraq is against Iraq's national interests. This principle is encapsulated in the Transitional Administrative Law, which states: "Armed forces and militias not under the command structure of the Iraqi Transitional Government are prohibited, except as provided by federal law."

200. In practical terms, we continue to work at integrating personnel from existing militias into Iraq's emerging national security structures, including the Iraq Civil Defence Force, and the New Iraqi Army.

Reconstruction

The circumstances of the conflict in Iraq were particular: operations without broad international consensus in a country with a relatively advanced but extremely decrepit infrastructure. While MOD is right to assess whether a national capability to repair infrastructure is required, it would be wrong to assume that a capability which might have been useful in Iraq will necessarily be required in future operations. (Paragraph 422).

201. The MOD has contributed significantly toward the programme of infrastructure repair in Iraq. Of course, no two crises will be the same, and such events will often call for different sets of technical skills and capabilities. Whilst reconstruction efforts post conflict are not core military business, the flexibility and resourcefulness of British servicemen and women resulted in the adaptation of specialist military skills to ensure essential work was completed in Iraq.

202. Despite the different types of operations undertaken by UK forces, there are capabilities that have proven to be common to many post-conflict scenarios. A cross-government and, where possible, international approach to infrastructure requirements is key to ensuring that such objectives are met. In this broader context, a cross-departmental group is investigating ways of improving HMG's planning, coordination and management of post conflict reconstruction issues—this includes civilian (public and private sector) deployments in order to provide capability and harness relevant expertise.

Quick Impact Projects are, as one of our interlocutors told us in Iraq, a 'band-aid' solution, which cannot hope to approach the scale of the reconstruction effort required in Iraq. But they have been a vital tool for showing that there are immediate benefits from the presence of Coalition forces and the end of Saddam Hussein's rule. We commend all those involved. (Paragraph 425).

203. We agree that the Quick Impact Projects have been successful in making a visible difference in the post-conflict period. The most important effect was on the local civilian population, who benefited from investment of small sums in the areas of health, education, law and order, essential public services (sanitation, water, power) as well as some 'normality' of life (banks, transport).

204. By late November the British Army had planned or carried out 634 projects worth £9.4m. The smallest project—repairing an ambulance for a small community—cost £25. Around 40 projects have been worth £40,000 or more. The remainder have been smaller sums.

205. This has shown that the UK Services are fully committed to improving life at street level, as the larger reconstruction projects were being planned. The gaining of trust has been enhanced at relatively low cost, and the benefit has been to the UK military as well as the local population.

Coalition efforts to clear unexploded ordnance throughout Iraq will make the country a far safer place for the people who live there. But the failure to provide sufficient forces to guard and secure munitions sites in the weeks and months after the conflict cost

Iraqi civilian lives, and also provided potential enemies of the Coalition with a ready stock of easily accessible weaponry. (Paragraph 431).

206. The Divisional Explosive Ordnance Disposal (EOD) teams worked tirelessly to clear unexploded ordnance in the MND(SE) area of operations but the scale of the problem led to a contractor being employed to deal with the clearance of the 67 captured Enemy Ammunition (CEA) sites. Despite clearing between eight to 10 tonnes of ammunition per day by April 2004, 24 sites still remained. These sites were widely dispersed, generally poorly constructed and in some cases contained up to 1000 tons of often-unstable explosives, which had to be destroyed in situ. The requirement to secure these sites once they had been identified was well understood by commanders but with finite resources available, the guarding of these static sites had to reflect overall priorities. Where possible Iraqis were employed to release Coalition troops. It is estimated that at least six more battlegroups would have been required if MND(SE) were to physically guard every site, and this is simply not a realistic proposition.

The Government should look again at whether the relatively modest funds that it has dedicated to supporting the clearance of unexploded ordnance in Iraq are adequate for the task at hand. (Paragraph 432).

207. MOD committed a very large proportion of its deployable EOD capability to theatre. At its peak, this consisted of around 240 trained EOD personnel from all three Services and a significant number of additional Royal Engineers and others involved in securing and marking EOD sites. Together, they made a vital contribution to addressing the problems of explosive remnants of war (ERW) in Iraq; since the beginning of the conflict they have cleared around a million items of ERW. However, experience suggests that humanitarian ERW clearance is best funded through NGOs and commercial demining companies. Such organisations have years of experience of unexploded ordnance clearance in a wider range of situations than do UK forces. They also often have better contacts and, in working with local people, they obtain a far better picture of the problems and clearance requirements than our forces could alone. Funding for these bodies, which is administered by the Department for International Development, provides a faster and more needs-driven ERW clearance operation than could be performed by our Armed Forces alone.

Mistakes were made in identifying potential local leaders, and without better intelligence and a better understanding of Iraqi society, such mistakes were probably inevitable. (Paragraph 437).

208. The repressive nature of the Iraqi state ensured that there was no ready-made alternative leadership. The challenge of identifying political leaders was compounded by the fact that Iraq was a difficult intelligence target.

The Armed Forces have done their utmost to fulfil their responsibilities to the Iraqi people as the occupying power, and we applaud them. But they have been under-resourced for this enormous task. It is unreasonable to expect the military to have a fine-grained understanding of how an unfamiliar society operates; but without this understanding, and without substantial civilian support in the form of experts and interpreters to help them to gain this understanding, mistakes were bound to be made which would make it more difficult to construct the kind of Iraq that the Coalition

wants to see: stable, secure and prosperous; a threat neither to its neighbours nor to the wider world. (Paragraph 441).

209. Fulfilling the UK's responsibilities as Occupying Power is the responsibility of the Government as a whole and not only the Armed Forces. Approximately 400 civilian employees have been seconded to the Coalition Provisional Authority as the vehicle for discharging these responsibilities and the Government has committed £544 million to the reconstruction of Iraq. The Armed Forces have played a substantial role in the administration of Iraq, particularly in the provision of security. Whilst we of course acknowledge that there is always room for improvement in specific areas, we do not accept as a general proposition that the Armed Forces have been under-resourced for the task.

210. As noted previously, there are many activities underway across Whitehall to consider methods of better coordinating national efforts in conflict scenarios, for both the conflict prevention stages and for military-civilian transitions and post conflict reconstruction.

Information Operations

UK Psychological Operations Capabilities

Our evidence suggests that if information operations are to be successful, it is essential that they should start in the period when diplomatic efforts are still being made, albeit backed by the coercive threat of military force through overt preparations. This would allow for the full potential of information operations to be exerted in advance of the start of hostilities and might even contribute to their avoidance. (Paragraph 455).

211. We agree that as a general principle Information Operations should start as early as possible—with the aim of helping avoid hostilities, or, at the very least, minimising their intensity. This approach is firmly embedded in evolving concepts for Effects-Based Operations, which aim to integrate various effects in support of a strategic end-state. Each campaign is, however, unique, and the role of Information Operations in each will vary. Our pursuit of a diplomatic solution to the Iraq crisis meant that military preparations needed to be carefully measured. This was reflected in the themes and messages of the overall Information Campaign which operated in support of that approach.

Effectiveness

We believe that the British information operations campaign did not begin early enough. We are concerned that the lessons of the Kosovo campaign were not better learned in this important area. It is disappointing that the Coalition is widely perceived to have 'come second' in perception management. However, we recognise that 'coming second' may be inevitable if a conflict of choice is being pursued by liberal democracies with a free media. We are, however, persuaded that information operations are an activity which can be expected to become of increasing importance in future operations. There were a number of successes which provide evidence of the potential effectiveness of information operations. We recommend that the Government should consider significantly enhancing our capabilities in this area. (Paragraph 465).

212. We note the Committee's comments about timing. Like other military preparations, information operations have to be calibrated so as to support and not undermine diplomatic efforts.

213. It is true that an Information Operations campaign which transmits messages that are transparent, credible and true may have difficulties against authoritarian regimes that entirely control their media, and who are prepared to coerce, embroider or lie. This proved, at times, to be the case during Operation TELIC. Iraq's Information Campaign was, however, fatally exposed when independent news organisations were able properly to compare the regime's announcements with actual events. In this sense, and beyond the very short-term, the Coalition's Information Campaign prevailed.

214. More could, however, have been done to limit the regime's Information Campaign abilities, and at an earlier stage. We were, for example, at times unable to prevent, by technical means, the channels the regime used to communicate with the Iraqi population. Had we been able to, we would have denied Saddam publicity in the crucial early stages, whilst retaining the relevant infrastructure for the Coalition and Iraqis to use at a later date.

215. Information Operations are firmly established in the UK's military inventory. As we move further towards Effects Based Operations, we will continue to seek ways to further enhance our capabilities.

Role of the Media

We believe that the importance of the media campaign in the modern world remains under-appreciated by sections of the Armed Forces. The early establishment of a robust media operations capability in theatre must be a priority for any operation. Where an operation is perceived to be a 'war of choice' the ability to handle multiple media organisations in theatre with professionalism and sophistication is essential. (Paragraph 477).

216. We are disappointed that the Committee formed the view that the importance of the media campaign was under-appreciated by sections of the Armed Forces. The importance of media operations is regularly emphasised to military personnel, and has been fully recognised in both this and previous operations. Indeed, during this operation, unprecedented efforts were made in terms of the numbers of media operations staff deployed and the numbers of journalists embedded with the Armed Forces. The development of a robust and high readiness early-entry media capability, as part of the Defence Media Operations Centre continues apace. This work started some time before Operation TELIC.

We strongly believe that the live broadcast of the death of service personnel would be utterly unacceptable. We recommend that MOD begin discussions as a matter of urgency with media organisations to find a solution to this very real possibility in a future conflict. (Paragraph 480).

217. Continuing dialogue with the broadcast organisations has shown that this is just as much of a concern to them as it is to the MOD. Green Book War Correspondent arrangements give some measure of control. Some UK media organisations inserted a